DISCARD

ANIMAL EXPERIMENTATION

Cruelty or Science?

Revised Edition

ANIMAL EXPERIMENTATION

Cruelty or Science?

Revised Edition

Nancy Day

Enslow Publishers, Inc.

40 Industrial Road   PO Box 38
Box 398   Aldershot
Berkeley Heights, NJ 07922   Hants GU12 6BP
USA   UK

http://www.enslow.com

Library of Congress Cataloging-in-Publication Data

Day, Nancy.
    Animal experimentation: cruelty or science?/ Nancy Day—Rev. ed.
        p. cm. – (Issues in focus)
    Includes bibliographical references and index.
    Summary: Explores the debate over animal experimentation and
testing. Explains the theory behind animal rights and outlines
alternatives to animal experimentation. Also describes medical
breakthroughs that have come from animal experimentation.
    ISBN 0-7660-1244-1
    1. Animal experimentation—United States—Juvenile literature.
    2. Animal rights activists—United States—Juvenile literature.
    3. Animal rights movement—United States—Juvenile literature.
    I. Title. II. Issues in focus (Hillside, N.J.)
    HV4930 .D39   2000
    179'.4—dc21
                                        99-049334
                                        CIP

Printed in the United States of America

10 9 8 7 6 5 4 3 2 1

To Our Readers: All Internet addresses in this book were active and
appropriate when we went to press. Any comments or suggestions can
be sent by e-mail to Comments@enslow.com or to the address on the
back cover.

Illustration Credits: The American Anti-Vivisection Society,
p. 63; ASPCA, Warren W. McSpadden, p. 35; Cedars-Sinai
Medical Center, p. 79; Molecular Devices Corporation, p. 101;
National Archives, p. 88; National Institutes of Health, pp. 14,
26, 39, 56, 74; National Library of Medicine, pp. 44, 47; Peter
Orkin, p. 98; People for the Ethical Treatment of Animals,
pp. 11, 53, 70; School of Medicine, Loma Linda University,
p. 92; University of California, Davis, p. 51; Wyeth-Ayerst
Laboratories, p. 86.

Cover Illustration: National Institutes of Health.

Contents

Acknowledgments

Jonathan Balcombe, Ph.D., associate director for education, Animal Research Issues, The Humane Society of the United States; Neal Barnard, M.D., president, Physicians Committee for Responsible Medicine; Elizabeth Darrow, former intern, People for the Ethical Treatment of Animals; Murray Gardner, M.D., professor emeritus of pathology at the University of California, Davis, School of Medicine; Alan M. Goldberg, Ph.D., director, Johns Hopkins University Center for Alternatives to Animal Testing; Stephen Kaufman, M.D., co-chair, Medical Research Modernization Committee; Michael Kirby, Ph.D., director of Pediatric Research, Loma Linda University; Robert F. Phalen, Ph.D., professor of community and environmental medicine, College of Medicine, University of California, Irvine; Cindy Sardo, assistant director/communications manager, California Biomedical Research Association; Martin Stephens, Ph.D., vice president for Animal Research Issues, The Humane Society of the United States; John Young, V.M.D., director, department of comparative medicine, Cedars Sinai Medical Center; Stephen Zawistowski, Ph.D., senior vice president for operations, science advisor, American Society for the Prevention of Cruelty to Animals; special thanks to Robert Day, Betty Day, and Joe Sakaduski.

Author's Note

Since the publication of the first edition of this book, the subject of animal experimentation has remained extremely controversial. People on all sides of the issue forcefully defend their points of view, certain they are right and eager to convince others of their righteousness. New technologies such as embryo research, cloning, and the human genome project have complicated the discussion.

I have tried to make this book a balanced discussion of the subject, the issues involved, and the concerns of all sides. It was not easy. Wild claims, questionable photographs, unlikely explanations, and bald-faced propaganda are easier to come by than hard facts when it comes to the subject of animal experimentation.

Sadly, the violence and threats that people and institutions have experienced as a result of their activities in this area have, if anything, increased. Some researchers declined to be interviewed, others refused to provide photographs or agreed to provide them only if they could do so anonymously. Companies and institutions were particularly frightened of repercussions.

The people who agreed to be interviewed and to give their names and affiliations should be respected for their willingness to go public on this volatile subject. They are taking a risk, making themselves vulnerable to criticism and retaliation, because they believe it is essential that you understand this issue.

Increasingly, the animal experimentation propaganda war is focusing on students. In school and out, you will undoubtedly see and hear a great deal on this subject. Take the time to analyze the claims. Ask yourself whether arguments make sense. Do your own research. Visit animal shelters, hospitals, and research centers. See for yourself how research is conducted and what the results of that research are. Think. Then make up your own mind.

1

The Battleground

Free The Animals!
—title of a book by Ingrid Newkirk,
National Director of People for the
Ethical Treatment of Animals (PETA)

B$_y$ 2:45 A.M., everyone was in place. They carried black shoulder bags for their booty and syringes filled with a drug called ketamine hydrochloride. They had staked out the location for weeks. They knew the guard's schedule. They knew when police cruisers drove by. A key street light had been darkened by a well-aimed BB gun. It was Christmas 1982.

The words "unit test only, unit test" came over the walkie-talkies. That was the signal to move. The group made its way out of an alley, across a narrow street, to the door. One member attached suction cups to the thick glass panel on the door. Then he quietly etched out a square of glass with a diamond-tipped pen. It made a popping sound as he removed it. Their hearts beat faster. There was no turning back now. The raid had begun.

The group included two surveillance vehicle drivers, two people to break in, two to carry the loot out, a transfer vehicle driver, and two support people. They even had someone to call if they needed money to bail them out of jail.

The leader of the group had been trained to break into buildings, change license plates, forge driver's licenses, and disable police cars. She had been taught the Ninja method of controlled movement, the art of disguise, and various surveillance techniques. All her preparation was about to pay off—but not in money. For the group was not breaking into a big-city bank or even a treasure-filled mansion. They were breaking into a building owned by Howard University in Washington, D.C. It was a research laboratory. And they were breaking in to steal cats.

The group worked quickly and efficiently. First they injected the cats with ketamine hydrochloride, an anesthetic, to make handling easier for the cats. Then they scooped up cat after cat, leaving in their place a copy of an animal rights book. Everything went like clockwork. The whole operation took less than forty minutes.[1]

Alan Hermesch, the spokesperson for Howard University at that time, had the job of dealing with

The leader of the group that conducted the raid on Howard University (in disguise to avoid identification).

the press the next day. He estimated the loss at $2,640, including property damage. The laboratory had been using cats to research the effect of drugs on the nervous system. In the past, animal experiments at the lab had helped researchers discover a way to tell whether someone has sickle cell anemia. (Sickle cell anemia is a life-threatening blood disease with no known cure.) The cats that the group had stolen had been bought from a supplier of laboratory animals, according to Hermesch. They had been at the lab for less than a month.[2]

The activists said that the cats were bone thin

and that some had broken bones or surgical cuts. One cat had died. The activists were outraged. "Animals feel pain," said Anjo (not his real name), a member of the Animal Liberation Front (ALF), the group responsible for the raid. "They have a right to a decent life with members of their own group." The activists were proud that they had given the cats a Christmas gift of freedom.

One of the Howard University researchers, who had been studying nerve injuries in cats, lost a year's worth of research in the raid. For that researcher, it was no Christmas present.[3]

It is difficult to determine how many animals are used for research, but experts agree the number is declining. The most recent comprehensive report, issued in 1986, used U.S. Department of Agriculture (USDA) data to estimate that 17 to 22 million animals were used in research and testing in the United States in 1983.[4] Jonathan Balcombe of The Humane Society of the United States estimates that between 15 and 20 million vertebrate animals are currently used each year in the United States and between 60 and 80 million are used worldwide.[5]

In the United States, records are kept only for animals covered by the Animal Welfare Act. According to the USDA's Animal Welfare Enforcement Report, 1,267,828 of these animals were used by registered facilities for research purposes in the United States in 1997. The preliminary estimate for 1998 was 1,214,000. The species used were an estimated 27,000 dogs, 25,000 cats, 57,000 primates, 261,000 guinea pigs, 206,000 hamsters,

288,000 rabbits, 158,000 farm animals, and 143,000 other animals.[6] These numbers, however, do not include the most common laboratory animals: rats and mice. This group represents another 12 to 18 million animals. Most sources agree that the use of animals for research peaked in the 1970s and has dropped by as much as half since that time, with the largest drop being in the use of cats and dogs.

Researchers use animals for experiments because animals' bodies often react in ways that are similar to the ways in which human bodies react. Sometimes scientists use small samples of tissue, cells, dead animals, or computer models instead of whole, living animals. But in some cases a living system is necessary, scientists say, to get accurate results from the experiments. For example, a drug may have side effects that could be seen only in a live animal.

Animal research proponents say that almost every major medical discovery in the last hundred years has involved experiments on animals. Without animal experimentation, they say, medical progress would grind to a halt and science would be set back centuries—this at a time when there is tremendous pressure to find treatments for diseases such as AIDS and cancer.

Animal rights activists do not agree. They say that animal research is ineffective. Where are the cures for cancer and AIDS, they ask, if animal research has been so worthwhile. The advances of the past are due more to research on humans, and improvements in living conditions, than animal experimentation, according to this view.

Rats and mice are the animals most commonly used to conduct basic research.

Many animal activists are opposed to animal experimentation on moral grounds. One of the largest animal rights groups in the country, People for the Ethical Treatment of Animals (PETA), has as its motto "animals are not ours to eat, wear, experiment on, or use for entertainment." Chris DeRose, founder and president of Last Chance for Animals, another animal rights organization, puts it simply: "I'd give my own life to cure cancer. I don't, morally and ethically, however, have the right to kill a single rat; I don't care what preposterous justification they try to use."[7]

Animal research proponents say the morality is in saving human lives. They point to the millions of people whose lives have been saved or improved through research on animals.

Between these two positions is a vast sea, influenced by tides of public opinion, government regulation, cultural differences, and ethical considerations. Most people agree that some guidelines or regulations should control animal experimentation. But where should the line be drawn? And who should draw it? If we stop allowing animal experimentation, should we also outlaw eating beef and wearing leather shoes? If we allow experimentation on monkeys and apes, does that mean we should allow experimentation on humans who do not have the mental capacity to understand what is happening to them? What about the terminally ill? The old and senile?

The battle between scientists and animal rights activists continues to heat up. According to the Justice Department, there were 313 acts of animal rights terrorism committed from 1977 to 1993. The Animal Liberation Front (ALF) has been identified as the main instigator for crimes such as break-ins, vandalism, theft, and arson.[8] A spokesman for PETA calls the extremists' actions valuable but points out that most of the work done in support of animal rights is in the form of education, outreach, and lobbying for legislation.

In recent years, individual researchers have been targeted—almost in the same way abortion providers have been singled out by antiabortion activists. Colin Blakemore, a professor of physiology in England, has had his cars vandalized, seen the windows of his home smashed by a masked mob, received two letter bombs, and been threatened, demonstrated against, and assaulted. He is one of several researchers reportedly marked for assassination by a militant animal rights group.[9]

Animal rights activists want to stop what they consider needless animal suffering and loss of life. Animal research proponents say that without animal experimentation, there would be needless human suffering and loss of life.

Do animals have rights that include the right not to be subjected to medical experiments? Do researchers have the right to conduct experiments that could provide a cure for AIDS or other diseases, even if it means death or discomfort for many laboratory animals? Activists are using advertising, the courts, public opinion—and even illegal actions—to make their case.

2

Science and Experimentation

Virtually every advance in medical science in the 20th century . . . has been achieved either directly or indirectly through the use of animals in laboratory experiments.
—American Medical Association (AMA) White Paper on the Use of Animals in Biomedical Research, 1992

Scientists use animals in medical research to study how the body works and how to diagnose, cure, and prevent disease. Researchers also use animals for tests to try to protect the public from dangerous chemicals. When live animals are used, this practice is called vivisection, a word that originally meant cutting, or performing surgery on, a living animal.

17

Animals in Research

Sometimes scientists use primates—monkeys and apes—for research because they are so similar to humans. But other times scientists use animals that appear very different from humans. Mice and rats are often used because they are cheap, have short life spans, and can be bred to have certain characteristics that make them suitable for particular experiments. Scientists select a particular animal because something about the animal makes it attractive for a particular type of study.

The Watanabe Rabbit

One day in 1973, Yoshio Watanabe of the University of Kobe in Japan noticed that one of the rabbits he was tending had yellow, fat-filled nodules on its feet. Watanabe discovered that the rabbit had an extremely high level of cholesterol in its blood. Realizing how valuable such an animal would be to researchers studying cholesterol, Watanabe began to purposely breed a line of rabbits with high blood cholesterol.

Watanabe rabbits suffer from a rare genetic defect that causes fatally high levels of cholesterol in the blood, a condition similar to a disease humans get called familial hypercholesterolemia. Children with the disease usually die of a heart attack before they reach their teens.

Watanabe rabbits were used in the development of an artificial liver that is used to cleanse the blood of children with familial hypercholesterolemia. The rabbits also played an important role in research on cholesterol that opened up new areas of drug research.[1] The authors of that study, Michael Brown and Joseph Goldstein of the University of Texas, were awarded a Nobel Prize in 1985.[2]

For the scientists studying the effects of high blood cholesterol and for families of children with familial hypercholesterolemia, the value of the Watanabe rabbit seems clear. Yet this line of rabbits was created, by humans, from a biological fluke. And the rabbits were bred to be experimented on and then to die.

Is it fair to create a life that is fatally flawed? Do humans have a right to create animals for their own use? Researchers, animal rights activists, experts on medical ethics, and critically ill people who are awaiting research breakthroughs each have their own point of view.

Animal Models

Scientists studying a particular body process or disease use experimental animals that model, or display the characteristics of, that process or disease. Sometimes, the best model is an animal that suffers from the same disease as humans. These are called spontaneous models. Animals that are used for research because they are spontaneous models include:

    dogs—hemophilia (excessive bleeding)
    mice—epilepsy (a condition that causes seizures)
    rabbits—glaucoma (an eye disease)
    cats—deafness

Even though these diseases and conditions can occur naturally, research animals are often bred to intentionally produce afflicted animals.

Researchers also use induced models. These animals were once normal. Scientists inject chemicals, microorganisms, or other substances into the animals to produce a particular disease or to create symptoms that mimic a specific condition. An example of an induced model is the armadillo, which is used for research on Hansen's disease (formerly called leprosy).

Scientists studying body structures or functions look for animal models that have characteristics that make examination easier. For example, a lot of the research on human vision was done on horseshoe crabs because they have large eyes with simple, accessible structures. Dogs are used for certain kinds of studies because their organs are similar in size to humans.

Animal activists question whether any animal is a good model for human disease. They say that it is better to study the disease in people who already have the disease than to use animals that get another form of the disease or may react to it in different ways.

The Experiment

Experimentation is an essential part of the scientific method used to gain knowledge. A scientist using the scientific method gathers facts, develops a theory, uses experiments to test the theory, and then alters the theory based on the results of the experiments. Throughout history, experimentation has been the distinguishing feature of science. Benjamin Franklin flying his kite during a thunderstorm to prove that lightning is electricity is a famous example.

A good experiment is designed so that every factor that could possibly affect the outcome is controlled, or fully known, except one. That one uncontrolled factor, the experimental variable, is the factor being studied. In the natural world, there are many factors that can affect a process or result. Scientific advance must rely on controlled and well-designed experiments to determine which factors are crucial and which are not.

The importance of controlling variables is both a reason for and a reason against using animals for experimentation. On the plus side, animals are often less complex than humans in both mind and body. They can be used in great numbers because they are readily available. Effects on future generations can be studied in animals with short life cycles. Their diet, environment, and even their genetic makeup can be controlled. On the negative side, animals are whole, living beings. Unlike a chemical in a test tube, it is impossible to control every variable and remove every element of unpredictability. Their bodies may act and react differently than human bodies. And animals cannot communicate their feelings and reactions the way humans can. Side effects such as headache, nausea, and depression may be difficult to detect in animals.

Another requirement of scientific experiments is

that they be reproducible. That is, other scientists should be able to repeat the experiment, using the same methods and materials, and get the same result. Scientific knowledge is not established until the results of an experiment have been repeated by other researchers. Experiments are repeated many times by many different scientists.

Scientists are often criticized by animal activists for repeating experiments, thereby using many additional animals. Sometimes experiments are repeated to reproduce, and therefore validate, another scientist's work. Other times they may be repeated for demonstration purposes. Repetition also occurs when scientists do not know that experiments have already been done. Some people have suggested establishing a nationwide data bank of information on animal experiments so that experiments are not needlessly repeated. In the area of product testing, duplication of experiments results from different companies creating and testing their own brands of products, testing to assure the safety of each batch of products, or extensive testing to protect the company in the event of a lawsuit.

How Animals Are Used

Animals are used in experiments for three general purposes: to find out how biological systems function or what factors affect behavior; to educate and train students in medicine and science; and to test drugs, chemicals, or products to determine their safety and effectiveness. Experiments can range from simply observing the behavior of an animal to killing the animal to examine its tissues.

Although much attention is focused on personal care and household product testing, this use probably accounts for well under one percent of the animals used by laboratories. Diagnosis and education each account for less than 5 percent, toxicity testing (of other products) makes up approximately 10 percent, drug discovery and biologicals production accounts for 20 to 30 percent, and other types of research make up the balance.[3] However, it is difficult to be sure of the exact counts.

Basic Research

Basic research involves answering fundamental questions about biological systems. The questions are often quite specific. For example, scientists studying cancer may examine how a particular cell functions or how a certain gene works. Scientists often study particular diseases to learn more about how the disease works, what causes the disease, what can prevent it, and what might be able to cure it. Animals are used in research on vision, aging, the immune system, neuromuscular diseases, heart disease, AIDS, infectious disease, cancer, nutrition, dentistry, and diabetes, and in many other fields.

Behavioral research is directed toward finding out what factors affect behavior and how various organisms and organs respond. For example, dogs have been useful to scientists trying to understand the eating disorder, anorexia nervosa. Animals are used by scientists studying addiction, mental illness, communication, language, and many other areas. Basic research consists of small building blocks of knowledge that scientists hope will lead to a broader understanding.

Education and Training

Animals used for education and training range from frogs that are dissected in classrooms to dogs that undergo open-heart surgery to train surgeons. Although many of the animals used for education are already dead, they have been killed for that purpose.

Concern over limiting the number of animals used for education has led to the development of alternative teaching tools. These range from plastic models to video discs, charts, computer programs, and new approaches to learning about life processes.

Dissection is usually the first time students come face-to-face with the subject of animal experimentation. Virtually every American has been inoculated with vaccines made using animals, has used products tested on animals, and has taken drugs developed using animals. However, it is one thing to use hairspray or get a vaccination without thinking about how the products were tested and another to be holding a scalpel and staring down at the naked belly of a frog.

Neal Barnard, M.D., president of the Physicians Committee for Responsible Medicine (PCRM), a group that opposes animal experimentation, calls dissection an archaic practice. "Frankly," he says, "I think it was archaic when I was in school thirty years ago. We're not trying to train kids to be veterinary surgeons. . . . The whole point of it [dissection] is to teach very, very elementary anatomical relationships. . . . I just think that there is no argument for dissection whatsoever. . . ."[4]

Barnard says that the use of animals for education is declining. For trauma training in medical schools, says Barnard, instructors are starting to use cadavers (dead bodies) instead of live animals. "And if you use a human cadaver, you have perfect anatomy." According to Barnard, about three quarters of the 126 medical schools in the United States had animal laboratories just a few years ago, but fewer than half of them have animal labs now. And of those, only one makes student participation mandatory.[5]

Many students, caught in the middle, are confused. Elizabeth Darrow worked for a year as an intern at the Washington headquarters of PETA, one of the largest animal rights groups. "Before I became aware of animal rights activism," says Darrow, "in seventh grade I dissected a fish, a worm, and a sheep's eyeball. I found it absolutely fascinating. But then when tenth grade dissection rolled around and I had become interested in animal rights activities, I talked to my teacher and asked if this was really necessary. Unfortunately, she wasn't very sympathetic. But there was another biology professor at my school who was sympathetic and he had obtained all the computer programs and alternative methods to dissection, which I used, and actually

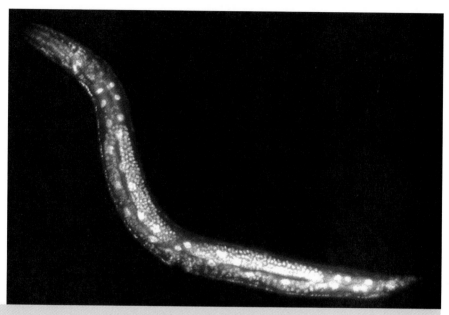

Science students dissect all kinds of living things at school, including worms.

found that I learned an incredible amount more from doing computer dissection and reading up about anatomy rather than actually dissecting an animal."[6]

Although some educators and scientists believe that dissection can actually increase a student's understanding and respect for all living beings, some students find that the reverse is true. "I thought it was very cruel," says Darrow. ". . . I saw all these dead animals—dead frogs lying on the dissection trays—and how wrong I thought that was that we had killed this animal to dissect it, and how little most of the students were learning."[7]

Some scientists and educators say that dissection

is an essential part of science education. They say that dissection has a hands-on value, that students learn the basic principles and practices that govern all the sciences, and that they develop an appreciation for the contributions of animals to science history and medical progress.

Critics of dissection say that it hardens students and desensitizes them to the cruelty involved with animal research.

Product Testing

Primitive humans may have fed unfamiliar plants to animals to see if they were safe to eat. Today, most new drugs, chemicals, household products, cosmetics, and other materials are tested on animals (or are made from ingredients that have been tested on animals). Materials are tested on animals to determine whether they work (in the case of drugs) and are safe.

Toxicity testing, or testing to determine whether a substance is poisonous, involves a wide range of tests to determine how the substance is absorbed, how it reacts in the body, and how the body reacts to it. Animals are exposed to the chemical through inhalation (breathing), ingestion (eating), eye contact, or skin contact. Most chemicals are tested in two or three different species of animals. How the chemical reacts may vary by species, sex of the animal, age, and other factors. Differences are carefully noted and may indicate the need for additional testing. Tests are also performed to determine whether the substance harms the animal's ability to reproduce or whether it causes birth defects in the offspring. Long-term tests, such as those to see whether the substance causes cancer, take two years to complete. Other tests, such as those to determine eye and skin irritation, are relatively short term.

One of the biggest problems with toxicity tests performed with animals is determining what the test results mean for humans. What kills a mouse may be safe for a human and vice versa. Animal tests can also be insensitive or unable to correctly identify all of the positive results. Still, most of our information about a new chemical's potential risk to humans comes from animal tests.

One of the best known—and until recently most used—toxicity tests is the LD-50 test. Groups of animals are given varying doses of a test substance. The dose that kills 50 percent or more of the animals is considered the lethal dose. This test has been largely replaced by one that uses fewer animals to determine estimates of toxicity. The Food and Drug Administration (FDA) does not require LD-50 testing to establish toxicity and encourages tests that do not use whole animals.[8]

Eye Irritation Testing

In 1933, a woman bought a new mascara called Lash Lure to darken her eyelashes. Soon after she used it, her eyes began to burn. Then her eyes ulcerated (developed sores); she went blind and eventually died. To prevent such a thing from happening again, the government enacted the federal Food, Drug and Cosmetic Act of 1938. Although it did not require specific tests, it was intended as a step toward protecting the public safety.

Scientists have studied eye irritation using animals since the 1920s. In 1944, FDA scientist John Draize came up with a scoring test to provide a way to evaluate a substance's irritancy factor. There is also a skin irritancy test that uses a Draize scoring system. The Draize eye irritation test involves putting the test material into one eye of each test animal. Any reactions to the material are scored using the Draize scale. The scores determine whether the product should be used near the eyes and what warnings should appear on the package.

Animal rights activists say the rabbit eye irritancy test is cruel and unnecessary. They feel that no animal should have human products, irritating or not, put into their eyes.

Stephen Kaufman, M.D., is chair of the Medical Research Modernization Committee (MRMC), a group that is critical of animal testing. He is also a practicing ophthalmologist who does not think that the eye irritation test is useful. "It's looking at the toxic effect on rabbits in an effort to assess irritancy in humans." He points out that the rabbit's eye differs from the human eye in several ways, including the fact that rabbits have a third membrane that may trap compounds in the eye. He says there are other ways of testing toxicity than the Draize test. "Not only is its reliability questionable but it has actually been shown to correlate poorly with human eye irritancy."[9]

Due to pressure from animal rights groups as well as the need to develop cheaper ways to evaluate eye irritancy, the cosmetic industry has contributed more than $100 million over the past ten years to develop alternative testing methods.[10]

Products that use cultured human cells and the CAM (chorioallantoic membrane) test, which uses a chicken egg instead of an eye to test chemicals for toxicity, are being used as alternatives or adjuncts. Tests such as Eyetex, which can screen a new chemical for possible toxic effects to determine whether further study is required, have reduced the number of animals needed for testing.

Although the Food, Drug & Cosmetic Act does not require animal testing for cosmetics, the FDA's position is that "the use of animals is necessary to ensure the safety of cosmetic products."[11] Further, the FDA says that the Draize test is among the most reliable methods for evaluating the safety of products used in or around the eyes. Animal rights activists say that the FDA's policies are outdated and that alternatives are just as good or better than the Draize method.

Public concern over harming animals to make cosmetics has led some companies to use the issue as a marketing tool. Some apply stickers with claims such as "Cruelty Free," "No Animal Testing," or "Not Tested on Animals." These claims can be misleading because virtually all ingredients in health and beauty products have been tested on animals at some time by some company. Sometimes manufacturers buy ingredients that have been tested by another company. Other times, companies buy ingredients that have been tested on animals long ago and do not require additional testing. In 1995, the National Consumers' League recommended to the Federal Trade Commission (FTC) that animal testing labels be banned as misleading. In 1996, the FTC responded that they would not pursue the matter as no consumer injury results from the labels.

In 1998, Great Britain banned testing of cosmetic ingredients on animals. While animal rights advocates applauded the ban, they acknowledged that most British companies already buy ingredients from countries where animal testing is routine.

Developing New Drugs and Procedures

It takes an average of seven years to test a new drug before the FDA can approve it for the general public.[12] Animal research helps determine what the drug does to the body and what the body does to the drug. Tests are also performed to find out whether the drug causes any dangerous side effects and to determine its safety at different doses.

Only a few drugs that are tried on animals ever reach human testing. The number that actually end up on drugstore shelves is even lower. Estimates range from 1 in 2,000 to 1 in 10,000. After drugs have received FDA approval (based on animal tests), clinical trials, or controlled experimental use by humans, can begin.

People volunteer to try experimental drugs

because they hope to benefit from a new treatment or sometimes because they want to help scientists and health care professionals learn more about the benefits and side effects of the treatment being studied. Some animal testing continues in order to provide information about whether long-term use of the drug may cause cancer or birth defects and to uncover any new uses for the drug. Additional animal testing may be needed if the human tests uncover any unexpected results.

Some critics have questioned the value of testing new drugs on animals. Drugs shown to be safe for animals can turn out to be dangerous for humans. In these cases, they say, animal testing may lead to a false sense of security.

Regulations Protecting Laboratory Animals

The Animal Welfare Act of 1966 was the first U.S. legislation to control the use and treatment of laboratory animals. Since that time, a number of amendments have been added. The act sets minimum standards for handling, housing, feeding, and watering laboratory animals. It also establishes basic levels of sanitation, ventilation, and shelter from temperature and weather extremes.

The Improved Standards for Laboratory Animals Act of 1985 added several important provisions. The law requires researchers to consider alternative methods that do not involve animals and to consult a veterinarian before beginning any experiment that could cause pain. It also requires adequate care before and after surgery, including adequate pain relief. Dogs must receive proper exercise, and primates must have environments that promote their psychological well-being. Each registered research facility must appoint a committee to monitor animal research. The committee must include a veterinarian and a person not affiliated with the institution to represent the community's interest in animal welfare.

Animal activists have complained that although rats and mice account for 85 to 90 percent of the animals used for research, they are not covered by the Animal Welfare Act. In 1998, the Alternative Research and Development Foundation, a group affiliated with the American Anti-Vivisection Society, filed a petition with the United States Department of Agriculture (USDA), asking that rats, mice, and birds be covered under the Act. Many scientists say that the change would be costly and unnecessary, as the USDA has determined that 90 percent of the rats, mice, and birds used for research are already protected by voluntary accreditation or policies that require compliance with standards that often exceed those in the Animal Welfare Act.[13]

Pain

One of the biggest concerns surrounding animal experimentation is the issue of pain and suffering. Here, as in almost every other area of this issue, people disagree over the facts. According to the USDA, 54 percent of the animals used in experiments in 1995 experienced no pain or distress.

Thirty-seven percent were used in experiments involving pain, but the pain was alleviated through medication; 8.8 percent were involved in experiments in which they experienced pain but no pain relief was given.[14] In some of these cases, pain relief could not be given because the research involved the study of pain.

Animal advocates challenge these figures. They note that the numbers are based on information provided by the researchers themselves, not by any outside source. They also say that the figures do not account for psychological pain, and question whether scientists accurately report the numbers and types of experiments they conduct.

Some European countries, Canada, Australia, and New Zealand use pain scales to report animal distress. A 1995 report from the Netherlands indicated that 54 percent of animals had minor discomfort, 26 percent had moderate discomfort, and 20 percent experienced severe discomfort during experiments.[15]

Use of Pound Animals

According to The Humane Society of the United States, 8 to 12 million animals enter shelters (facilities for unwanted animals) each year and 30 to 60 percent are then euthanized (killed as painlessly as possible.)[16] Some estimates of the number killed run even higher.

For years, scientists got research animals from shelters or pounds. It was a cheap, plentiful source of supply. The feeling was that if the animals were going to be killed anyway, why not let them make a contribution to research that might save the lives of other animals or humans. Initially, humane societies cooperated with laboratories, providing animals that were going to be killed anyway. Then the public became concerned about family pets ending up in research laboratories.

In recent years, animal activists have fought to prevent or restrict the use of pound animals by medical researchers. In some states, pounds cannot provide animals to laboratories. Researchers who want animals must buy animals bred for research

Controversy has surrounded the use of pound animals for research purposes.

(which are considerably more expensive) or get pound animals from another state.

Scientists point out that if researchers are forced to buy specially bred research animals (many of which will end up being killed), more animals will end up dying. Robert Phalen, Ph.D., is a professor of community and environmental medicine for the College of Medicine at the University of California, Irvine. Phalen says, "We dispose of two hundred thousand pound animals a week in this country—and they're basically just killed and tossed. Biomedical research needs one week's worth of those for the entire year, and that's for developing new surgical techniques, for training paramedics, for training surgeons and nurses, and training medical students."[17]

Many of the organizations that provide shelters have opposed the use of such animals for research. They feel that their duty is to provide a place for people to take their unwanted pets where there is a hope of them being adopted. Even if the animals end up being killed, at least the pet owners know where and under what conditions the animals die.

3

The History of Animal Experimentation

Vivisection is monstrous. Medical science has little to learn, and nothing can be gained by repetition of experiments on living animals.
—Sir George Duckett, Society for the Abolition of Vivisection, 1875

Animals have been used in research for more than two thousand years. In the third century B.C., Erasistratus of Alexandria used animals to study body functions. Galen, who was born in A.D. 129, is considered the founder of experimental physiology. He used animals to prove his theory that veins carry blood, not air. However, because he studied only apes and pigs, he made many errors when

37

he transferred his knowledge to humans. Dissection of human bodies was prohibited at that time, so Galen's errors went undetected for hundreds of years. His mistakes were corrected in 1543 when Vesalius published his *Seven Books on the Structure of the Human Body*, which was based on actual human dissections.

Opposition to animal research has been present in Europe for more than four hundred years. René Descartes (1596–1650) defended the practice, saying that animals lack the ability to think and reason and therefore are like machines. But another philosopher, Jeremy Bentham, disagreed. He said that humans and animals are linked by their common ability to suffer and their common right not to suffer and die at the hands of others. Bentham is remembered most for a passage he wrote in 1789 that is still quoted today: "The question is not can they reason? nor, can they talk? but can they suffer?"[1]

Bentham introduced the utilitarian argument against animal experimentation. This argument holds that one should act in a way that brings about the best balance of good and bad results for every being affected.

Carolus Linnaeus, who developed a system for classifying plants and animals, put apes and humans in the same grouping. Although he noted that humans were different in their mental abilities and moral sense, "It is remarkable," he said, "that the stupidest ape differs so little from the wisest man, that the surveyor of nature has yet to be found who can draw the line between them."[2] Whether or not

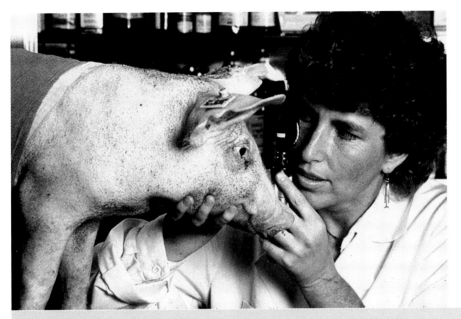

Researchers believe that organs from animals may be able to save many people's lives in the future.

humans are considered a higher order to be given special consideration is a key point in the discussion of animal experimentation.

The seventeenth and eighteenth centuries were a time of scientific revolution. Anyone could buy books, instruments, and specimens for their own experiments. Scientific demonstrations became a popular form of entertainment. These exhibitions sometimes involved cutting open live animals without anesthesia, which caused public objections. By the early part of the nineteenth century, animal research became an organized, systematic part of science, and opposition to it became more vocal.

The Antivivisection Movement

Animal protection laws began to be passed in Great Britain in the 1820s and 1830s. The laws were designed to protect animals from being used in bloody sports, such as bullbaiting and dogfighting, and from being forced to pull overloaded cabs. People at the time condemned cruelty as an act connected with bad character. The notion that cruelty is demeaning to humans is an argument that was dropped in later years in favor of the idea that animals have an intrinsic, or basic, value.

People who argue against the use of animals in research began to split into two groups. Moderate humanitarians were willing to balance human and animal interests. The other group was against any kind of experimentation on animals. This separation can be seen today as the difference between animal welfare advocates (people who believe that animals should receive humane care and treatment) and animal rights advocates (people who believe that animals have rights that include the right not to be experimented on or used by humans for their own purposes).

Some criticism of animal research came from within the medical profession itself. Marshall Hall (1790–1857), a British scientist, proposed five principles of animal research. He believed that an experiment should never be done

1. if the information could be gained by observation,

2. without a clearly defined and attainable objective,

3. if it is an unnecessary repetition of previous experiments,

4. if it is not carried out with the least possible suffering,

5. if every physiological experiment cannot be witnessed.

Without these laws to regulate research, Hall thought that physiologists would be seen as cruel.

In 1865, Claude Bernard published *Introduction to the Study of Experimental Medicine*. He intended to give physicians rules and principles to guide them in their studies. Bernard thought of the laboratory as the "true sanctuary of medical science" and considered it much more important than the study of patients. He popularized the use of animal models. In particular, he emphasized the importance of controlling all factors and studying a single variable.

On May 4, 1875, the founder of the British Antivivisection Society presented the first antivivisection bill in history before the House of Lords in Great Britain. During that same year, a provivisection group formed that later worked to protect experimentation on animals. On May 12, 1875, the Scientist's Bill was presented to the House of Commons. Intended as a compromise, it proposed regulation of painful experiments only. Scientists could apply for a license to conduct painful experiments. Pain was allowed if suffering was kept to a minimum, if it was for the purpose of a new discovery, and if anesthesia might change the results of the experiment. Parliament passed the Cruelty to Animals Act of 1876, which in addition to regulating experiments involving pain, prohibited the use of animals to practice surgical skills. It remained in effect until it was revised in 1986. It allowed painful experiments if they advanced physiological knowledge.

Vivisection and opposition to it were rare during this period in America. There were a few brief battles in the state of New York and the cities of Boston and Philadelphia around 1870. In 1883, the American Anti-Vivisection Society (AAVS) was founded. American research laboratories grew in number through the 1880s and 1890s, and the United States became a major center of science and medicine.

By the late 1800s, experimental medicine had gained support within the British medical profession. This was a period of spectacular medical advancements. Although many successes were due to improved hygiene and better public health programs, other advances resulted from animal research. By the 1900s, the perceived benefits of animal experimentation began to turn public opinion in favor of animal research.

Research-oriented science was largely supported and accepted by the American public during most of the twentieth century. The prestige and reputation of medical research scientists grew. The medical profession was well organized and had government support. After state anticruelty laws were passed, the humane movement reached a truce with scientists. Animal experimentation could continue as long as scientists promised to treat animals humanely.

In the late 1940s, pound seizure laws were enacted. These laws forced the release of unclaimed dogs and cats from pounds or animal shelters to medical research institutions for experimentation. The numbers of animals used in research had been climbing.

In 1959, a book was published that included what has become a goal for modern animal experimentation. The book was *The Principles of Humane Experimental Technique*. Its authors, W. M. S. Russell and R. L. Burch, proposed the "Three Rs" of humane experimentation: reduction, refinement, and replacement. These goals aim to reduce the number of animals used in experiments, to refine the methods of animal experimentation so that suffering is minimized and the knowledge gained is maximized, and to find other methods to replace the use of animals.

A survey by the International Committee on Laboratory Animals in 1959 reported that 17 million rodents and rabbits were used each year for research. By 1965, the number was estimated at 60 million. Government funding of research had increased. Some people began to get concerned. And the humane movement got involved. The uneasy truce between the humane movement and animal researchers that had lasted for forty years was over.[3]

In the 1960s, there were congressional hearings about the treatment of laboratory animals. A number

Galen dissecting a pig (A.D. 1565). Most of Galen's knowledge of anatomy came from animal rather than human dissection, which explains some of his errors.

of cases of abuse of dogs at the hands of dealers who sold to laboratories had been publicized. The hearings focused on the British Cruelty to Animals Act as a possible model for laws in the United States. A pro-research advocate noted that the vast majority of advances in surgery since 1876 had come from the United States and other countries, not from England. He argued that the act had restricted scientists and blocked their progress. T. Abel, vice president of the Royal College of Surgeons in London, responded: "We do not commit the atrocities which are reported from time to time in some other countries. . . . We have proved that the desired results can be obtained by less inhumane methods."[4] The resulting legislation in the United States was the 1966 Laboratory Animal Act.

The 1970s brought substantial change. People became concerned about the environment, social issues, and ethical problems. Then, in 1975, a book was published that would provide a strong voice against animal experimentation: *Animal Liberation* by Peter Singer.

Singer's book transformed the antivivisectionist movement into a movement for equal consideration of all sentient creatures (animals that are capable of sensations such as pain). Arguing from an intellectual, moral point of view, Singer brought back the utilitarian concept of finding the best balance of good and bad consequences for every being involved.

Since the 1970s, activists have shifted from promoting animal welfare to advocating animal rights. People who promote animal welfare want to regulate but not eliminate animal experimentation. Animal rights advocates are usually against any form of animal experimentation, and most are vegetarians who are against killing or using animals for any reason.

New Technology Raises Questions

In 1992, a thirty-five-year-old man was near death. His liver had been destroyed by the hepatitis-B virus. He was not eligible to receive a transplanted human liver because doctors thought the hepatitis would destroy the new liver too. But there was a liver that might be resistant to the disease—a baboon's liver. A healthy young adult baboon was killed and its liver transplanted into the man's body. Five days after the surgery, the man was up and about.

Unfortunately, he died after two months. Some people felt that the operation had been a breakthrough. If nothing else, perhaps animal organs could serve as "bridges" to keep patients alive until human organs became available. Others were shocked. Would animals now be seen as a source of spare parts for humans?[5]

Xenotransplantation, the use of live nonhuman animal cells, tissues, or organs in human patients, has become a major area of research, but it is not new. John Young, director of the department of comparative medicine at Cedars Sinai Medical Center, points out that "most of the people that are walking around today with transplanted heart valves have pig valves in their heart. That's a xenotransplant . . . We have been for many, many years taking tissues from animals and implanting them . . . in human beings." Young says that Cedars Sinai has also treated patients with liver failure using a bioartificial liver. A pig's liver that has been broken down into individual liver cells serves as a human liver by filtering the patient's blood. A new pig's liver is required every twenty-four hours for the procedure. Young reports that of fifty patients treated, forty were able to be kept alive until a human liver became available and are now doing fine.[6]

Could xenotransplantation be dangerous? Critics say yes. They point to the fact that many of the viruses that affect humans started as animal viruses. Examples of viruses that spread from animals to humans include HIV, Ebola, and "Mad Cow Disease." If an infected animal's organs were used in a human transplant, the virus could potentially cross the species barrier and spread to humans. Although these critics acknowledge that researchers use germ-free animals, they question how it would be possible

TAB· VI· 🐱 FELIS, ET LEPORIS· 29

Comparison of the speech organs of the cat and rabbit, from Giulio Casserio, De Vocis Auditusque Organis Historia Anatomica *(1601). Detailed studies of animals helped scientists understand many body functions and processes.*

to screen donor animals for viruses not yet identified.[7]

Young admits that the risk of transmitting viruses between species is a concern, but emphasizes that most xenotransplantation research is being conducted with species, such as pigs, that are less likely to carry viruses that can affect humans. He thinks that "we should proceed cautiously, under controlled situations, and extensively evaluate the outcomes of what we do . . . If every time a new technology came about people said, 'Oh, there might be adverse consequences, therefore we should abandon it,' I hesitate to think where we'd be today in practicing medicine."[8]

Could pigs save the lives of the ten Americans a day who die while waiting for organ transplants? Already, specialized farms are raising pigs that have been injected with human DNA, in an attempt to reduce the possibility that their organs would be rejected by the human body. Pig to human transplants have not yet been approved by the FDA, but pig to baboon transplant experiments have been promising.[9]

Another new breakthrough that has raised ethical questions is cloning. Scientists in Scotland were able to create a nearly identical twin by taking a mammary cell from the udder of an adult sheep and joining it with another sheep's unfertilized egg, which had first had its genetic material removed. The mammary cell provided the genetic material and the cell was able to grow into an embryo without ever being fertilized by a male. The embryo was implanted into the uterus of a sheep where it matured into a normal sheep that was nearly identical to the sheep from which the mammary cell was taken.[10] Some people fear this may lead to cloning humans. Others see it as yet another example of humans manipulating animals for their own benefit.

Organizations

Public interest in animal welfare is high. The animal protection movement's annual fund raising now amounts to an estimated $200 million.[11] The oldest groups have been around for more than one hundred years: the American Society for the Prevention of Cruelty to Animals (ASPCA) and the American Anti-Vivisection Society (AAVS). Other groups include the Fund for Animals, the Friends of Animals, and the Animal Protection Institute of America.

Two groups that have used a scientific approach to opposing animal research are the Medical Research Modernization Committee (MRMC) and the Physicians Committee for Responsible Medicine (PCRM). The MRMC was formed in 1978 and has eight hundred members, three hundred fifty of which are medical doctors. The PCRM was formed in 1985. It takes a broad-based activist approach promoting vegetarianism and alternatives to animal and human experimentation, as well as dealing with other medical issues.

People for the Ethical Treatment of Animals (PETA), with five hundred thousand members, opposes all forms of animal exploitation, including using animals for food, clothing, entertainment, and experimentation. Their efforts are targeted at swaying public opinion through protests, advertising and public relations efforts; at programs geared toward students; and at changing laws through lobbying, litigation, and government involvement.

A new development is the "straight edge" movement, consisting of younger, more radical members, who demand immediate action. These activists are more likely to become involved with the Animal Liberation Front (ALF). This group is listed as a domestic terrorist organization by the Federal Bureau of Investigation. Since 1996, ALF and a related group, the Earth Liberation Front, have been responsible for at least seven arson fires.[12] ALF has an estimated two thousand official supporters, but authorities say only about one hundred individuals actively participate in the group's activities.[13]

In recent years, animal welfare organizations such as The Humane Society of the United States (HSUS), which has 1.75 million members, and the ASPCA have become more resistant to animal experimentation. HSUS now has as one of its missions, "to reduce and eventually eliminate harm to animals used in research, testing, and education, through the promotion of alternative methods and other means." Although most humane groups do not oppose animal research categorically, many have actively fought against using pound animals as research subjects and have worked toward regulating research procedures and practices.

Groups that support the use of animals in

A $4.6 million arson fire at the University of California, Davis, Veterinary Diagnostic Laboratory, was attributed to animal rights activists.

research include the Incurably Ill for Animal Research (iiFAR), two thousand five hundred members, an organization of people who have health problems and are concerned that animal research will be stopped or limited due to the efforts of animal rights activists; the American Medical Association (AMA) with two hundred ninety-seven thousand physician members; the American Association for Laboratory Animal Science (AALAS) with eight thousand two hundred members; and Americans for Medical Progress (AMP) with three thousand members.

These groups are only some of the many organizations involved directly or indirectly with the subject of animal experimentation.

4

The Ethical Issues

All animals are equal, but some animals are more equal than others.
—George Orwell, *Animal Farm*

There are many different arguments for and against animal experimentation. Emotion runs high, and hard facts are difficult to find. Do humans have a right to experiment on animals? Do animals have rights of their own? If experimentation is to be allowed, which animals and what kinds of experimentation should be permitted? If controls are to be set, who should set them and why? It is like a slippery slope. Once you take a step back, you start to slide down. There is little to grab on to and no firm footing.

Discrimination by Species

One of the frequent points of discussion is whether the species of animal makes a difference. Anyone who watches a mother gorilla hold her baby or sees chimpanzees interact can tell that these animals are very much like us. That is why scientists use them in medical research . . . and why some people think they should not.

Humans and chimpanzees have in common at least 98.5 percent of their DNA. In fact, humans and chimpanzees are so similar in genetic structure that physiologist Jared Diamond has called humans "the third chimpanzee."[1] Is it all right to experiment on an animal that is so similar to humans?

Monkeys and apes are very similar to humans. Their closeness to humans has been used both as a reason for and a reason against using them for research.

If primates are not acceptable, what about dogs? Rats? Fruit flies? Viruses? Where should the line be drawn, and who should draw it? Animal rights activist Steven Zak questions whether we should treat dragonflies the same as dolphins, but suggests that even if one thinks that dragonflies do not qualify for rights, it seems wrong to crush one for no reason.[2] In a letter to the journal *New Scientist*, Geoff Kirby wrote, "Why are we not stirred by the deaths of creepy-crawlies . . . when are we going to be honest about 'animal rights' and offer the same respect to slugs as to seal pups?"[3]

Some people suggest that membership in a moral community puts humans above other animals. The natural world is violent, haphazard, and unfair. Lions do not wonder whether it is right to kill a baby zebra. Most animals appear to lack the capacity for moral judgment. Yet animal rights advocates suggest that if animals lack moral judgment of their own, perhaps they deserve consideration from us. If we have moral judgment, they say, why do we experiment on animals that have no power to resist? Does that show good moral judgment?

Another measure that has been suggested is intelligence. Humans have shown a superior degree of intelligence by developing language, making and using tools, being able to anticipate events, and being able to foresee the results of what they do. Ironically, it is this very intelligence that allows us to give informed consent, something animals cannot do. Informed consent is considered an essential part of medicine. It is a person's right to know, understand, and agree to a medical procedure.

Many animals show signs of superior intelligence and use language; some even use tools. Yet the abilities of most humans in these areas are far above those of other animals. In the last few thousand years, humans have created a culture rich with art, music, literature—and scientific knowledge. Animals do not build such an extensive heritage from one generation to the next.

Although intelligence appears to be a good measure of what might be acceptable in animal experimentation, it cannot be used as the only guideline. For example, would we allow experiments on people with low mental ability? And what about infants who appear to have little understanding of the world around them and no grasp of language? Raymond G. Frey, Ph.D., speaking at a 1996 conference on the ethics of animal research, argued that there is no characteristic shared by all humans and only humans that animals do not also have.[4]

Peter Singer, a professor of philosophy who has written extensively on animal rights issues, has suggested that sentience is a better criterion than species. Sentient creatures are conscious of sensations (such as pain) and respond to them. A difference of species is not a good distinction, Singer says, because acting purely on the basis of species is no different than acting solely on the basis of sex or race. The word animal rights supporters have created to describe such thinking is *speciesism*, or discrimination against other species. Sentience, says

Most experimental animals are rodents—primarily rats and mice—because they are cheap, readily available, reproduce quickly, and are good models for many studies.

Singer, is a more relevant guideline because it distinguishes animals that can feel pain.[5]

If we use sentience on an individual basis (not just by species of animal), then we must consider patients in comas (a state of deep unconsciousness) and people who have been declared brain-dead. Then there is the problem of being sure that they do not feel pain. And why should we use the ability to sense pain as a measure when, according to government statistics, most animal experimentation does not involve pain?

Tom Regan, a professor of philosophy at North Carolina State University who discusses animal rights issues, has used lifeboat scenarios to discuss ethical issues involved with weighing the interests of animals and humans. Suppose, says Regan, a lifeboat contains four healthy humans and a healthy dog. It is overcrowded and about to sink. Someone must be thrown overboard. Who should it be? Regan suggests that it would not be wrong to throw the dog overboard, not because the dog is not human but because its life is less rich in terms of possible sources of satisfaction. If the situation were changed, he says, and one of the humans was in an irreversible coma, the dog should stay and the comatose human should be thrown overboard. Regan considers the potential for a fulfilling life a justifiable guideline for making ethical choices.[6] Many animal rights advocates disagree.

The Greater Good?

Yet another ethical consideration regarding animal experimentation is whether the decision should be made based on the balance of good over bad. If enough good comes from experimentation, then does that outweigh the harm it causes the animals? Suppose a young child needs a heart transplant and the only match is an elderly man's. Is it right to kill the old man so that a child, who has his whole life ahead of him, can live? Does the end justify the means?

Jeremy Bentham argued that the suffering of animals does not outweigh the good for humans. Peter Singer and others argue that the suffering of animals is worth as much as the suffering of humans and therefore the results of animal experimentation are more bad than good. Yet the strongest argument animal research advocates have is the "greater good" that has come from it. They believe that if one weighs all the human and animal lives that have been saved or improved through animal research against the harm caused to research animals, the balance is clearly on the side of animal experimentation.

Is Animal Experimentation an Environmental Issue?

EnviroLink, which bills itself as "the Online Environmental Community" (found online at http://www.envirolink.org), says that it is "dedicated to providing you with the most comprehensive, up-to-date environmental resources available." Included in its community is the Animal Rights Resource site. Is animal rights an environmental issue?

The EnviroLink site contains information on Earth Day and promotes organic soaps, but through the animal rights site, it also provides information on an organization that supports the illegal activities of the underground group, ALF. Part of the information the group offers is how ALF members who have committed crimes can send information about their acts to get publicity (for example, type on plain paper in block letters, wear gloves to avoid fingerprints). Is this the sort of activity someone with environmental concerns should support?

Doug Inkley, a lobbyist for the National Wildlife Federation, accuses animal rights activists of "muddling" the issues so "they can ride on the coattails of the conservation movement, which is well supported by the American public."[7] Others who support animal experimentation say that the biggest threat to animals is not medical research but loss of habitat. Some animal rights activists say that conservationists want to save animals only so they can later be used for their own purposes. Conservationists say that animal rights activists are wasting their time trying to protect individual animals when whole species are being wiped out.

Would animal rights activists be better off fighting to stop the loss of rainforest habitat, where most of the world's species reside, or working to stop experimentation on animals in laboratories?

Animal activists say that people who care about protecting endangered animals and preserving natural areas should also want to save animals from being experimented on. They look at eating deer, wearing fur, experimenting on chimpanzees, and driving animals into extinction as examples of human greed, insensitivity, and lack of respect for the rights of animals.

5

The Case Against Animal Experimentation

Animal liberationists do not separate out the human animal so there is no rational basis for saying that a human being has special rights. A rat is a pig is a dog is a boy. They're all mammals.
—Ingrid Newkirk, National Director, PETA, as quoted by Katie McCabe

"Whenever I hear anyone arguing for slavery, I feel a strong impulse to see it tried on him personally." When Abraham Lincoln said those words on March 17, 1865, many people had just begun to see that it was wrong to use African Americans as tools and to treat them as property.

The Moral Argument

There are many animal activists today who see a strong comparison between research animals and slaves. These activists, like Lincoln, sometimes think about what it would be like to turn the tables—even for a moment. How would scientists like to have a new chemical put in their eyes to see if it is irritating? Would researchers be willing to receive head injuries so that new treatments could be tried out? Would a medical company president use his or her own child to train sales representatives to use a surgical stapler?

Are animals the slaves of our generation? Benjamin Lay, an eighteenth-century Quaker, once kidnapped the child of a slave-holding neighbor. He wanted the parents to feel the anguish of separated slave families. Is there any reason to assume that a baby monkey does not feel the same misery and fear that a human baby would when it is taken from its mother and locked in a steel cage?

Some people say that if research animals are similar enough to humans that they can serve as research substitutes, then they should not be experimented on. As philosophers Hugh LaFollette and Niall Shanks point out, this conflict makes some researchers uncomfortable with using chimpanzees for experiments. "The same feature that apparently makes them good test subjects also makes them too close to humans for moral comfort."[1]

Perhaps animal activists are ahead of their time. Maybe every animal is entitled to the same respect each human being expects. If so, we may one day look back—in the same disbelieving way we now look back on slavery—and say: "Can you believe what they used to do to animals?"

Questioning Animal Experimentation

Stephen Zawistowski, Ph.D., recalls his experiences with animal experimentation in college.

> I was a laboratory animal caretaker. I had to take care of the rats and the frogs and everything. I remember sending the frogs off to physiology lab, pithing [piercing at the base of the skull] twenty-five or thirty of them in the morning and sending them off to the physiology lab . . . I started questioning my own feelings on doing some of this stuff and how I wanted to go about the balance of my career. I actually ended up going to graduate school and spending all of my time working with fruit flies and blow flies. I was comfortable with doing research and experimentation on flies.[2]

Neal Barnard, M.D., recalls his upbringing.

> I grew up in North Dakota, eating animals, shooting animals . . . serving burgers at McDonald's. Before I went to medical school, I did animal experiments in college. . . . But I came to see that the animals, although they were humble animals, rats and pigeons—unpopular—they clearly suffered. . . . These [experiments on] animals could have easily been replaced but were vigorously defended by the people who had responsibility for them. And those two themes have continued to be in evidence when I've looked at this issue: that animals clearly suffer and the people who are in charge or who sponsor

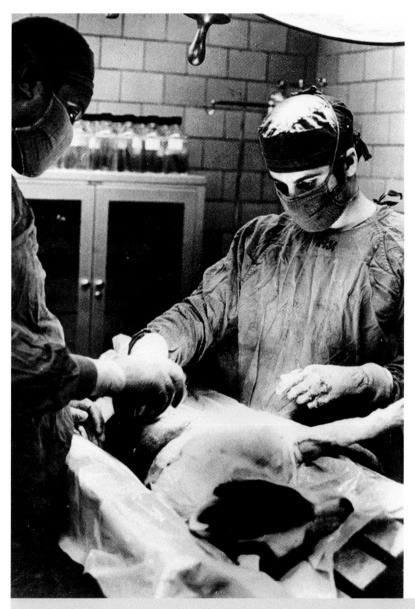

Dogs are used for research, education, and training. Most are killed afterward.

experiments defend them in spite of other ways of doing things being available.[3]

Stephen Kaufman, M.D., chair of the Medical Research Modernization Committee (MRMC), has similar memories.

> In high school, I worked in a lab. I saw a lot of things that disturbed me at the time, instances that could best be described as gratuitous cruelty . . . there were animals that underwent repeated surgeries that should have been euthanized, they were in pain, they were suffering . . . That sort of thing can affect you.

In medical school, Kaufman became even more concerned—not just with ethical issues but with what he saw as the questionable medical value of animal experimentation.

> To me, all of a sudden, more and more it seemed to crystallize that this doesn't even make sense in the first place. . . . Regardless of whether you care about animals, regardless of whether this violates some notion of rights or some notion of justice for animals, it doesn't even make sense scientifically.[4]

Animal Experimentation Is Misdirected

Critics of animal experimentation say that the current system of medical research, which relies heavily on animal experimentation, is focused on the mechanisms of disease, not prevention. Yet many of the leading causes of death in the United States (heart disease, stroke, cancer) are often lifestyle-related.

According to animal rights advocates, our entire healthcare system is based on making money by diagnosing and treating patients. If people practiced preventive medicine, had good dietary habits, exercised, and controlled their levels of stress, they would not be as likely to become ill. But there is little money to be made in preventive medicine.

The use of animals in research on preventable diseases also brings up another moral issue: Why should animals suffer for our lack of self-control? For example, is it fair to purposely get animals addicted to drugs in order to study treatments for addiction? And just because Americans eat the wrong things, smoke, do not exercise, and are under too much stress, should animals be made to do the same things just so we might learn more about our bad habits?

Critics also say that focusing on animal testing delays discoveries and draws scientists away from other research tools, such as epidemiological studies (human disease statistics), clinical observation, autopsy studies, and imaging technology. In an article for *Scientific American*, Barnard and Kaufman said, "although animal experiments are sometimes intellectually seductive, they are poorly suited to addressing the urgent health problems of our era, such as heart disease, cancer, stroke, AIDS, and birth defects."[5]

Animal Experimentation Is Unnecessary

Critics of animal experimentation question whether animals are really needed for medical research. They point to the many alternative methodologies that have been developed and question whether animal experimentation has provided any benefits that could not have been obtained through other means. For example, despite decades of research on cancer (much of it using animal models), the disease continues to be a leading cause of death.

The critics also challenge claims that most modern medical advances resulted from animal experimentation. The advances, say the critics, involved animals only because laws require that new drugs, procedures, or treatments be tested on animals first. This does not necessarily mean that the breakthroughs would not have occurred without the use of animals, they say. For example, claims that animal experimentation was vital in the under-standing and treatment of diabetes are unfounded, say Barnard and Kaufman. Human studies in the eighteenth and nineteenth centuries first revealed the importance of pancreatic damage in diabetes, studies on humans led to the 1869 discovery of insulin-producing islet cells, and "although cows and pigs were once the primary sources for insulin to treat diabetes, human insulin is now the standard therapy, revolutionizing how patients manage the disease," say Barnard and Kaufman.[6]

Another claim critics of animal experimentation dispute is that animals are needed so that scientists can control their experimental variables. Barnard does not buy that excuse. "It's in my mind, very much like the person who drops their keys on a dark street," says Barnard. "They can't look around there, they'd have no control over their search for their keys, so they go to the next street over, which is very brightly lit and they can search there very, very, well—they never find their keys—but they have terrific control over their method."[7]

Animal Experimentation Is Misleading

Animal activists say that animal experimentation has actually done more harm than good. Barnard says, "Animal tests have caused a very substantial loss, in terms of loss of money, in terms of the loss of good minds being devoted to a very, very limited methodology, and in terms of indicating that certain things are true which weren't true." As an example, Barnard points to the debate over cigarette smoking and cancer in the early 1960s.

> The people who felt that cigarettes were not the cause of lung cancer had a terrific piece of evidence on their side and that was that any time that experimenters had taken tobacco smoke and forced animals to inhale it chronically, the animals do not develop lung cancer.

The connection was proven by looking at epidemiological data—information on what actually happened in the human population—says Barnard. "Animal experiments were clearly leading people in the wrong direction. If that was an isolated episode, I wouldn't be perhaps so concerned, but it isn't."

"Anyone who asks the question, 'could we live without animal experiments,' I think is asking the wrong question," says Barnard. "The way to put it is: 'We know that animal experimentation is a very seriously double-edged sword. Granted it gives you data, but it gives you a lot of bad data.' "[8]

Critics of animal experimentation say that animals get different forms of diseases, experience diseases differently, or have conditions that seem similar but have different causes. Therefore, trying to understand human disease by using animals is difficult. Kaufman says,

> The likelihood that the animal results will accord with the truth in humans is very low, rendering animal model systems very unreliable, frequently misleading, and on balance so confusing that a strong case could be made that the research shouldn't be done in the first place.[9]

Overuse, Misuse, and Abuse

In 1981, police raided Dr. Edward Taub's Institute for Behavioral Research in Silver Spring, Maryland. They had seen a videotape, taken by PETA founder Alex Pacheco, who had posed as a lab volunteer for four months. The videotape showed unsanitary lab conditions, monkeys with unbandaged wounds, and other signs of abuse. The tape is hard for most people even to look at. As a result, the Silver Spring monkey case became a rallying point for animal activists.[10]

Activists are angry about the abuses that have taken place in research laboratories and the fact that medical researchers appear to be above the law. Zawistowski explains that in New York state the ASPCA has a law enforcement division with officers empowered to enforce laws governing the welfare of animals. Yet New York, like almost every state, has an exemption for agricultural and laboratory animals. "The simple fact is there are things you can do to a cow, a chicken, or a rat in the laboratory that, if you did that to your dog or your pet, we could summons you and arrest you."[11]

Criticism of Scientists

Many animal advocates view medical research as a profit-making industry and say that the profit motive leads to overuse and abuse. Kaufman explains:

> I think that, although people who work with animals claim that they do it only because they have to, what happens in the world of science is that there are certain things that are rewarded. The ultimate reward is getting grants. Because the issue has become so polarized, professors stress that animal research is valuable and overstate the case. This inspires students to pursue those careers [ones that involve animal experimentation], and once they start a career, they are locked in. That's where the grants are and that's where they will be successful.[12]

Zawistowski says that it is hard to get scientists to recognize that concerns over animal use are legitimate questions that deserve debate.

> The AMA [American Medical Association] reminds me of the NRA [National Rifle Association]. The NRA had that wonderful slogan on their car bumpers for awhile that said, "You'll get my gun when you pry my cold, dead fingers from around it". . . the AMA sounds a lot like that except "you'll get my rat when you pry my cold, dead fingers from around its body" because there is that kind of a knee-jerk reaction at any attempt to raise

questions about the use of animals in research and the way they're being treated.[13]

Why Oppose Animal Experimentation?

For animal activists, animal experimentation is not just a controversial subject—it is a matter of life and death for millions of innocent animals.

Elizabeth Darrow says, "I don't think we have the right to kill or use an animal for any reason, whether humans will benefit or not. I believe there are alternatives, and unfortunately, our medical industry has really been geared towards the use of animals and experiments."[14]

One of the monkeys that was taken from Dr. Taub's laboratory in Silver Spring, Maryland.

Animal activists who have seen evidence of past abuses suspect that similar abuses continue to go on but are never reported. Barnard says,

> I have come to the conclusion that researchers are very, very often tempted to stray into unethical types of research, not only on animals but on humans as well. . . . The whole idea that researchers have some tremendous ethical restraint and some tremendous vision and that they don't want to hurt animals but they only do so for the betterment of humankind I think is absolutely nuts.[15]

6

The Case for Animal Experimentation

Without animal research, medical science would come to a total standstill.
—Dr. Lewis Thomas, scholar-in-residence, Cornell University Medical College

The list of discoveries and technologies that have been attributed to work with animals is too long to name. The short list includes vaccines, antibiotics, anesthetics, insulin, cancer drugs, heart drugs, most surgical procedures, organ transplants, and the CAT scan.

Animal Experimentation Is Essential to Modern Medicine

Since 1901, sixty-five of the eighty-eight Nobel Prizes awarded in physiology or medicine have been for discoveries and advances that involved the use of experimental animals.[1] Some examples are studies using dogs on the connection between cholesterol and heart disease (1985), studies using chickens that linked viruses and cancer (1966), and the successful culture of the virus that causes polio (1954).[2] A 1996 poll of all living Nobel winners in the field of medicine found that every one of them agreed that the use of animals in research has been and continues to be vital to medical progress.[3]

When Jack Botting and Adrian Morrison made the case "Animal Research is Vital to Medicine" in a printed debate for *Scientific American*, they stated, "We cannot think of an area of medical research that does not owe many of its most important advances to animal experiments."[4] They described dozens of vaccines and antibiotics, open-heart surgery, kidney dialysis, organ transplantation, insulin for diabetes, and many other treatments and procedures that were developed using animal experimentation.

Meet the Scientists

Robert Phalen is an animal researcher who considers himself an animal welfarist.

> I think the spectrum of caring about animals includes three broad categories. [At one extreme are] people who are completely indifferent to animals . . . who don't care about animal feelings or animal welfare. At the other extreme is the animal rightist. . . . In the middle, where I see all of the scientists I know, is the animal welfare

"Nude" or hairless mice have unusually weak immune systems. Human cancer cells implanted in nude mice continue to grow, so scientists can study cancer in them without risking human lives.

group. An animal welfarist believes that animals can suffer and that suffering is bad and that we have an ethical obligation to reduce it and in fact work on techniques for identifying and reducing suffering.[5]

Phalen uses computer models, cell culture systems (systems that use human or animal cells), and isolated chemical systems, but he relies on animals to study the subtle effects of chemicals on body processes such as the immune system.

Murray Gardner, M.D., professor emeritus of pathology at the University of California, Davis, School of Medicine, is one of many scientists working to find a cure for AIDS. He uses macaque monkeys to study simian AIDS, which is similar to the AIDS disease humans get. The monkeys are required, according to Gardner, because they "sit between test tubes and humans." He says it is essential that AIDS drugs and vaccines be tested on animals before they are tried on humans.[6]

Michael Kirby, Ph.D., is director of pediatric research for Loma Linda University in California. He uses rats, cats, and monkeys to test procedures for helping premature babies. Some of Kirby's work involves experiments with liquid ventilation, a process that lets people whose lungs are damaged or underdeveloped due to prematurity breathe a special liquid. "The turnaround has been in the lives saved," says Kirby. "It used to be that babies that were twenty-four weeks or younger, down to twenty-one weeks, they all died. Now the vast majority of them are staying alive."[7]

Recently, Kirby's research has led to a technique that uses radiation to treat macular degeneration (a severe eye disease) in the elderly. The existing treatment often destroyed the patient's vision, while the new technique preserves it. He says, "The importance of using the animals was, number one, to make sure it was safe." Also, he says he had to determine whether there were any harmful side effects. "That's why the animal use was so critical," he says. "We just couldn't do it any other way."[8]

Animal Experimentation in Context

Throughout our history, animals have been looked on as a renewable resource for clothing, transportation, food, labor, and companionship. The use of animals in medical research was a logical extension of the practice of using animals to serve human needs.

Worldwide, billions of animals are killed each year for food. According to the National Agricultural Statistics Service, over 631 million cattle, sheep, hogs, chickens, and turkeys are killed in the United States alone each year for food production.[9] Animals are also killed for animal food, fiber production, to protect crops and other food sources, to clear land for development, and to keep houses free of pests.

Phalen suggests that we view biomedical research in perspective with our other relationships to the animal kingdom. As an example, says Phalen,

> the boy that lives next door to me can go to a pet store (he's twelve) and buy any animal and do anything he wants, and he has no standards in housing, medical care, or anything else. Whereas if I want to purchase one mouse for an inhalation toxicology test for a substance that physicians feel will save the lives of neonates [newborn babies] in our intensive care ward, I have to go through an animal care and use committee, and they determine . . . that the study is not frivolous . . . that I am qualified to do the study . . . that the methods are modern . . . that the animal number is minimized . . . if there's pain—more than a simple injection—the animals have to be rendered incapable of feeling that pain . . . that all the housing, transportation, and feeding of the animals

will be under the care of a veterinarian . . . and on and on. . . . In agriculture . . . animals are killed. There's no anesthetization or anything. In pets, there are no ethical standards. . . . I think the one that is leading the way, in my opinion, in terms of the ethical treatment of animals, is biomedical research.[10]

Some say that animal activists have targeted medical research because the benefits of animal research are not well understood by the public, and scientists are less able to defend themselves than larger and more powerful groups. The public is more likely to protest something that few of them understand than something, like eating meat, that most people accept. Yet scientists say that medical research is the very area where the greatest good has come at the smallest ethical price. Discoveries made through the use of animals have long-term benefits, they say. Unlike the pig that died for a pork sandwich, the pig that was used to create insulin helped prolong the lives of people with diabetes.

Animal Experimentation Helps Animals

According to scientists, humans are not the only ones to benefit from animal research. Many of the surgical techniques, diagnostic procedures, and medical treatments developed for humans can also be used to benefit animals. In addition, animal research helps scientists learn more about animal diseases and conditions.

Animal research has led to vaccines for rabies, distemper, anthrax, tetanus, and feline leukemia.

Open-heart surgery, pacemakers, and procedures to remove cataracts (an eye condition that affects vision) are all available to animals thanks to animal research. As a result, the lives of pets and farm animals have been extended and improved.[11]

John Young, V.M.D., director of the department of comparative medicine at Cedars Sinai Medical Center, is board-certified as a laboratory animal veterinarian. He sees his role as an advocate, or representative, for the animals.

> That's why I'm here. I became a veterinarian because of my love for animals. One of the things that you learn when you go through veterinary school is that everything that we know today and everything that we are learning today about veterinary medicine was learned in animal research. So not only am I advocating the welfare of the animals that are in my facility today, in the long run, animal health will benefit in general. . . .[12]

Animal Experimentation Must Continue

What would happen if all animal experimentation was stopped? According to a 1986 report to Congress by the U.S. Office of Technology Assessment, "Implementation of this option would effectively arrest most basic biomedical and behavioral research and toxicological testing in the United States." The report goes on to warn that the economic and public health consequences "are so unpredictable and speculative" that that course of action should be considered dangerous.[13]

Murray Gardner's research on AIDS using

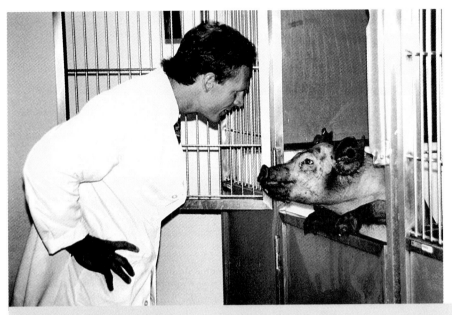

Laboratory animal veterinarian John Young considers himself an advocate for the animals on which he experiments.

macaque monkeys has led to the development of a vaccine that seems to provide some immunity to the simian version of AIDS. AIDS, says Gardner, is a "tough nut to crack," but animal research will be an essential part of finding a cure. Although it is certainly not 100 percent, Gardner says the vaccine gives a "glimpse of hope" to AIDS patients.[14]

Some scientists say that people with incurable diseases would have less reason for hope if animal research were halted. Much research would stop, and patients would not have the benefits of medical advances. They would be exposed to the unforeseen dangers of new treatments that were not fully tested in animals. Without animal models, a complete understanding of some diseases might never be achieved. If animal research on cancer had been restricted twenty years ago, more than half of the anticancer drugs in use today would not be available. Without animal research, millions of cancer patients around the world would be subjected to unnecessary suffering and early death.[15]

Proponents of animal research say that cancer would not be the only area to be severely affected. There would be fewer new diagnostic techniques, surgical procedures, and treatments for many diseases and conditions. Dr. Michael E. DeBakey, pioneering heart surgeon, says, "As a human being and physician, I cannot conceive of telling parents their sick child will die because we cannot use all the tools at our disposal. How will they feel about a society that legislates the rights of animals above those of humans?"[16]

Criticism of Animal Activists

"I think animal rights groups have exerted fruitful pressures in improving care and maintenance," says Walter Freeman, a professor who uses animals in his research. "But some groups are halting research altogether."[17]

Kirby received a letter calling him a Nazi and was picketed for his research. "We've had to install safeguards," he says, "to prevent people from breaking into our labs. That's a use of costly funds that otherwise could have been used for research." Kirby acknowledges that animal activism has produced some benefits.

> I think that the animal activists have been good to the extent that they have raised everyone's consciousness about treating animals. . . . Unfortunately, they have been extremely detrimental to research too. The mistruths and the outright lies that they have induced in the public media I think [have] distorted the public's concept of what really happens in research.

Like many scientists, Kirby thinks that most animal activists mean well.

> I think they're basically good people with good intentions, but they've been fed a lot of propaganda that is simply incorrect. . . . Now there are a few, the really fringe radicals, who can never be reached. These are the people, for instance, who equate the life of a rat to that of a human. And for those people, I really feel sorry. . . . I think anyone who's had a child, for instance, would say in an instant, take the rat's life if you could save my child.[18]

Why Support Animal Experimentation?

Virtually everyone has had vaccinations that were developed using animals, has taken drugs that were tested on animals, and may even have been saved by a surgical procedure, diagnostic test, or medical treatment discovered or tested on animals. "Without animal research," says Dr. Leon Sternfeld, medical director of the United Cerebral Palsy Research and Education Foundation, "the various types of preventive measures that we now have would not be possible."[19]

Musician Paul McCartney has been a vegetarian and vocal opponent of animal testing for many years. But when his wife, Linda, faced breast cancer and he learned firsthand about experimental cancer treatments, his opinion changed. "I am finding out now that there is quite a lot of animal experimentation—some of it, I suppose, absolutely necessary when you come down to final tests before people," he said.[20]

7

Experimentation on Humans

> *Morality rests on what is right in itself towards the individual immediately involved, not on justification by result, even though that may possibly benefit a great many others.*
> —M. H. Pappworth, author of *Human Guinea Pigs: Experimentation on Man*, 1968

One alternative to using animals for medical experimentation is to use human beings instead. If this seems shocking, keep in mind that human experimentation is already a very large and important part of medical research today. Human experimentation can range from a college student who gets paid twenty dollars to test different types of adhesive tape to a gravely ill cancer patient who agrees to try a new drug. Experimental drugs, therapies, and procedures are tried on human subjects all the time. However, strict guidelines are used to protect the experimental subjects.

Give Me Your Poor, Your Incarcerated, Your Terminally Ill

When in 1796 Edward Jenner wanted to test a new smallpox vaccine he had made from cowpox virus, he vaccinated his servants' children. Then he purposely exposed them to smallpox. Historically, scientists have first looked to the lower levels of society for experimental subjects. Critics say this willingness to experiment on those who are less powerful and less able to refuse participation parallels the use of animals for experimentation.

For hundreds of years, criminals were considered ideal subjects for experimentation. They are kept under the same conditions and fed the same food and have the same sleeping hours. As with laboratory animals, many variables can be controlled to assure more accurate results for the experiments.

Using prisoners for experimentation was outlawed in 1974, but before that time, the practice was widespread. Prisoners were used to test everything from toothpaste and shampoo formulations to mind-altering drugs and toxic chemicals.[1]

At one point, terminally ill patients were considered good research subjects. In the 1950s, there were several cases of patients with advanced cancer being used to develop procedures for X-raying organs. These procedures involved injecting dye into veins of the liver or spleen. Many of the patients had complications, some of which were severe. Physicians practiced on the terminally ill patients before testing the procedure on their other patients.[2]

Although terminally ill patients are no longer treated as research material, Dr. John McArdle, the scientific advisor to the American Anti-Vivisection Society (AAVS), has suggested using brain-dead humans instead of animals for surgical research. "It may take people awhile to get used to the idea," he admits, "but once they do, the savings in animal lives will be substantial."[3]

Children, particularly those considered impaired, have also been used for experimentation. In 1957, fifteen mentally impaired infants, ages two days to nine months, were used to determine the normal blood pressure in the pulmonary artery during the first few months of life. The doctors passed a catheter (a thin, flexible tube) through each baby's veins from the thigh through the heart and into the pulmonary artery. At the same time, they put a cannula (large hollow needle) into the artery of the other thigh. The infants were not given any sedatives.[4]

This study, which was reported in the *Journal of Paediatrics*, shows how differently children, particularly "defective" children, were viewed forty years ago. Now, parental consent is required before any experimental procedure or treatment is tried on a

"Conquerors of Yellow Fever," a painting by Dean Cornwell. Dr. Lazear allows an infected mosquito to bite Dr. Carroll to prove that mosquitoes carry yellow fever. Dr. Lazear also experimented on himself and died as a result.

child. Experiments that do not directly benefit the child involved are undertaken rarely, if ever.

People often point to the experiments performed by Dr. Josef Mengele on prisoners at the Auschwitz concentration camp during World War II as the ultimate example of medical experimentation gone wrong. Mengele's experiments on human beings, many of them children, included painful tests without anesthetics, needless amputations, the deliberate infection of wounds, mismatched blood transfusions, crude surgeries, injections of dye to change eye color, and other, even more bizarre procedures. He examined, then killed and dissected, twins, thinking it a wonderful opportunity to learn everything about their differences and similarities.[5]

Some animal activists see a parallel between the Nazi medical experiments and animal research. Mengele's "research" was so important to him that he saw the suffering involved as insignificant.

The Tuskegee Experiment

Next to the Nazi experiments, the Tuskegee study was probably the most infamous case of unethical experimentation. It was also the longest nontherapeutic experiment on human beings in medical history. From the beginning, the idea was to observe—not treat—sick people.

From 1932 to 1972, the United States Public Health Service, working with other health care providers and researchers, followed more than four hundred African-American men in Macon County, Alabama. The men were poor, uneducated, and unskilled. They suffered from syphilis, a sexually transmitted disease that leads to tumors, organ damage, bone deterioration, cardiovascular disease, severe central nervous system problems, and, often, death. The researchers wanted to know more about untreated syphilis. Specifically, they wanted to find

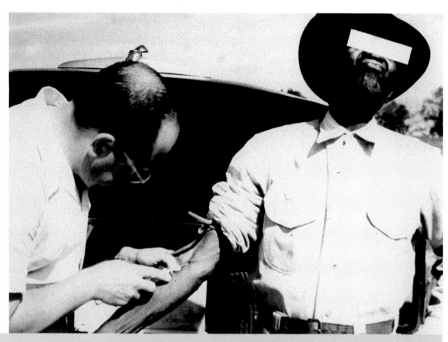

The men who took part in the Tuskegee experiment were subjected to blood tests and other procedures but their disease was never treated.

out whether syphilis was as damaging a disease to blacks as it was to whites.

Subjects underwent blood tests, X-rays, and painful spinal punctures. Few if any of the men understood the study, and many were deliberately misled. Years later, television reporter Harry Reasoner said that the experiment had "used human beings as laboratory animals in a long and inefficient study of how long it takes syphilis to kill someone."[6]

Although no legitimate researcher today would defend the way in which the Tuskegee experiment was conducted, it does bring out an uncomfortable moral issue that relates to animal research. Is it acceptable to use animals in experiments that might lead to improvements in the lives of humans or other animals if the experimental animals involved receive no benefit at all and often die as a result? Animal rights advocate Tom Regan would say no. He uses the example of a wealthy, but old and cranky, aunt. If he killed her, he would inherit her money sooner, and could donate a large sum to a children's hospital and help many people. Nevertheless, he points out, killing her—even if it benefits many other people—is not a morally acceptable choice.[7]

Secret Government Experiments

In December of 1993, U.S. Secretary of Energy Hazel O'Leary released secret government documents concerning radiation experiments on human subjects. The Energy Department documents showed that the department had conducted some eight hundred radiation experiments—mostly in the late 1940s and 1950s—on mentally retarded children, seriously ill patients, soldiers, medical students, and others.

At the end of World War II, American military officials—fearing nuclear war with Russia or China—were desperate for information on the effects of radiation. Even though it was well known that radiation is harmful, the effects of brief exposure, the speed at which radioactive substances would be cleared from the body, and the lasting damage radiation would cause were not fully understood.

In their frenzy for knowledge, the U.S. Atomic Energy Commission, NASA, and the Public Health Service approved radiation experiments on humans. Many of the experiments were performed on people who either did not know or did not fully understand the risks of radiation. Some were even performed without the patients' knowledge.

The experiments involved not only government workers but researchers at many of the country's leading universities and research centers. Newborn boys in four states were injected with a radioactive substance without their parents' permission. Retarded children were fed food laced with radioactive iron and calcium. Prisoners were irradiated and operated on. Medical students and hospital patients were injected with radioactive substances.

O'Leary felt that if Americans had been hurt or killed by the experiments, the government should accept responsibility. She also hoped that by lifting the veil of secrecy that has surrounded her department, she could prevent such a thing from ever happening again.

Experiments Using Human Embryos and Fetuses

Embryos and fetuses are of interest to scientists because they have characteristics different from adult organisms. Research using human fetuses was banned in 1988, but the ban was lifted in 1993. Fetal cells have been used to treat people with Parkinson's disease. While not a cure, transplanting fetal cells into the brains of Parkinson's patients helps restore motor function and reduces the need for medication.[8]

Should scientists be able to use human embryos and fetuses? Researchers use embryos created for infertility treatments but then not used, and fetuses that have been aborted. Is this a good use for human tissue that might normally just be discarded? Or does it devalue human life and perhaps open the door to the possibility of women becoming factories for producing fetuses for research?

One area of study involves human embryonic stem cells, master cells that produce cells destined to become brain matter, blood cells, organ tissue, or other body parts. Scientists studying embryonic stem cells discovered a way to direct the cells to make a particular type of tissue, introducing the possibility that scientists might one day be able to "make" human organs for transplantation. The discovery kicked off a host of new studies, which were halted when a number of groups protested experimentation on human embryos.

In 1995 Congress banned human embryo research. The ban forbids federal money (most research is funded with federal money) from being used for "research in which a human embryo or embryos are destroyed, discarded or knowingly subjected to risk of injury or death greater than that allowed for research on fetuses in utero."[9] Some claim that embryonic stem cell research may lead to new therapies for Alzheimer's disease and diabetes, as well as ways to help prevent birth defects and to

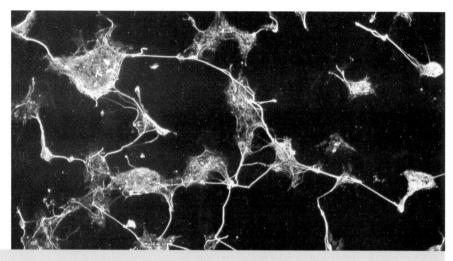

Rat fetus retinal cells are used to explore the genes that control brain development.

create or repair human organs. Others say that it is immoral to use human embryos for research.

In 1998, scientists using private funding created a line of embryo stem cells that can be grown in the laboratory to supply researchers. Although the cells originally came from human embryos and fetuses, the National Institutes of Health, the main provider of federal money for research, has stated that these cells are lab-grown, and therefore are allowable as a study tool.

Ironically, the use of embryonic stem cells could reduce the need for animal testing. By testing new drugs on these human cells first, only the safest candidates would then be tested on animals and eventually humans.[10]

Human experimentation came to a halt at Duke

University Medical Center in Durham, North Carolina, on May 13, 1999, when a federal watchdog agency pulled the center's license to carry out federally funded research. The agency, the Office for Protection from Research Risks (OPRR), said the center did not meet federal ethics rules. According to OPRR, administrators at Duke had failed to correct "serious deficiencies" in their procedures for monitoring patient consent and keeping records.

OPRR allowed Duke to resume experimentation. Four days later, after the center submitted a reform plan, the OPRR sent a message to federally funded research institutions. It said that the government would be keeping a close eye on studies that use human subjects.[11]

Clinical Trials

Before being approved for use in the general population, a new drug or procedure must undergo clinical trials—controlled testing on human subjects. Clinical trials, however, are the last step in a long process. A new cancer drug, for example, will first be tested on cells in a laboratory. If it kills cancer cells and seems to be safe for normal cells, the drug is then tried on animals, usually several different kinds of animals.

Only after a drug has been shown to be effective and safe on animals is it tried on a limited number of human volunteers through clinical trials. Clinical trials help determine the best dosage, or amount, of drug to give and the best way to give it. Sometimes the trials identify a new use for the drug.

Many drugs never make it beyond the clinical trial stage. Perhaps they do not work as well in humans as they did in animals. Or they may have unacceptable side effects.

A study released in 1998 was critical of pharmaceutical companies for attracting volunteers with advertisements offering free treatments or cash payments without also explaining the risks. The federal investigators conducting the study also said that patients participating in clinical trials were often exposed to unsafe and unethical practices because the research was not being properly supervised.[12]

Sometimes participating in a clinical trial can be risky even if the subject is a "control," a subject who undergoes the same procedure but is not given the actual substance being tested. Steve Ashworth had four holes drilled into his skull in hopes that he would be in the group getting an experimental fetal cell transplant. Instead, it turned out that he was a control. Ethics experts questioned whether having a patient undergo a phony surgical procedure was an acceptable risk, but the doctor who conducted the study said that it was vital to know whether the treatment was effective before trying it on thousands of patients.[13]

The number of clinical trials is growing, due to the increasing amount of research on cancer, AIDS, and other diseases. In addition, ten years ago it took an average of forty clinical trials to get a drug to market. It now takes sixty.[14]

Human Volunteers

In 1997, the Amvac Chemical Corporation had a laboratory in England give adult volunteers small doses of a pesticide called *dichlorvos* to see how much it reduced an enzyme in their blood. The enzyme, cholinesterase, affects brain and nerve cells. The volunteers were fully informed about the experiment and the tests had been reviewed by a medical ethics committee. Amvac then approached the Environ-mental Protection Agency about conducting similar experiments in the United States. Amvac and other pesticide manufacturers want to use human testing to gather data to support their view that controls on pesticides are too stringent.[15]

Should this kind of testing be forbidden? What if fully informed volunteers are willing to participate?

Researchers often struggle to balance patient rights with their need to assure the accuracy of the results. For example, what if it becomes clear before a study is complete that one of the drugs being tested on cancer patients is not working very well. Should the patients be told? Should they be allowed to withdraw from the experiment and seek other treatment? Another sticky area is the use of healthy volunteers to test experimental procedures. The patient does not directly benefit, but the research may help others.

Scientists such as Robert Phalen say that human experimentation could never substitute for animal experimentation. "Even if there were enough human volunteers," says Phalen, "animals would still have to be used. Animal research is necessary in areas [where] we truly can't use human beings." As examples, Phalen cites research on birth defects, studies on chemicals that may produce irreversible damage such as blindness, procedures involving changes in the brain, and experimenting with new surgical techniques.[16]

Philosopher Tom Regan also has concerns about the use of human volunteers. He warns that if scientists came to rely on healthy human volunteers who would be paid for participating, only poor and uneducated people would participate. Few affluent people would volunteer, says Regan.[17] Finding valid alternatives is the answer, he says. Many scientists would agree.

8

The Alternatives

The least we owe animals in laboratories is an honest effort to search out ways to minimize their suffering and use.
— Paul G. Irwin, president, The Humane Society of the United States

Perhaps the only thing that animal activists and animal researchers agree on is the need for accurate, inexpensive, simple tests that can replace animals with no added risk to public safety. The search for alternatives is based on the Three Rs of humane experimentation: reduction, refinement, and replacement.

Cell Cultures

Using animal or human cells, tissues, or organs for experimentation is not a new idea. However, their use has grown dramatically in recent years. This type of research is known as "in vitro" (in glass) to distinguish it from "in vivo" (in the living being). In vitro procedures are performed in test tubes, assay plates, or other glass (or, more commonly, plastic) containers. Artificial environments designed to simulate living systems are created using animal or human cells, tissues, or organs. Scientists also include bacteria, fertilized chicken eggs, and frog embryos under the category of in vitro testing.

Animal cells are used for a large number of in vitro tests because some human cells cannot be cultured in the laboratory. In addition, the supply of human cells is limited. Human cells usually come

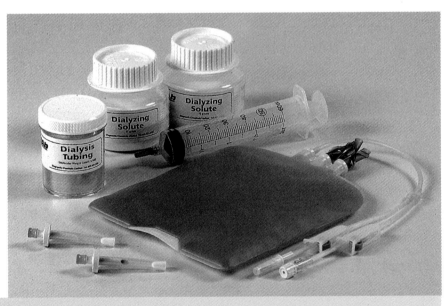

Used in place of mice in animal experimentation, the product i-Mab *uses a special bag to produce monoclonal antibodies.*

from tissue left over from surgery or from cadavers. When animal cells are used, a single animal can supply a large number of cells and many different kinds of cells.

Cell cultures are used in toxicity testing to help scientists evaluate the risk of certain chemicals. The dose of the chemical that each cell receives can be carefully controlled and measured. Only small quantities of the test substance are required—an important advantage where rare or toxic chemicals are concerned. Cultured organ cells can be used to predict toxicity in target organs, such as the liver, heart, kidney, and lung. Tumor cells can be used to screen new drugs to see whether they have any anticancer properties.

Cell cultures have their limitations, however. Cell cultures cannot evaluate whole-body responses such as changes in blood pressure or reactions from the immune system. Differences in routes of exposure— eating, breathing, or skin contact with the chemical—cannot be measured. Long-term exposure cannot be tested nor can the body's ability to repair any damage the chemical causes.

Sometimes, if cell cultures cannot be used, non-mammalian models can be. For example, scientists are beginning to use fish as replacements for mice and rats in some types of research. Sometimes, simpler organisms such as roundworms, or even microorganisms such as yeasts or bacteria, can be used for research.

New developments have made tissue culture an even more valuable tool for researchers. Michael

Kirby says he is using more tissue culture techniques due to advancements in genetics. "Now we're using a lot of tissue culture to look at the same issues we used to look at in the intact animal," he says. He notes, however, that animals are still needed to produce the tissue.[1]

Computer Programs and Mathematical Models

Computer programs can simulate a variety of biological functions and interactions. Some models use in vitro or animal data to predict whether a chemical might be toxic. Computers can also be used to maintain a database on chemicals so tests are not needlessly repeated.

According to the trade group Pharmaceutical Research and Manufacturers of America, it takes an average of fifteen years and $500 million to develop a new drug.[2] Computer-aided drug design may reduce the trial-and-error process. Computers can "virtually screen" millions of chemical combinations in search of potentially beneficial drugs. The selected compounds can then be "tested" on computer models of patients. Using computers to identify the best candidates for drug development reduces the number of animals needed for testing in the same way that using computers to simulate car crashes reduces the number of cars destroyed in real crashes staged for safety testing.[3]

Computer simulations are not perfect. The accuracy of the computer model depends on how

The Cytosensor™ Microphysiometer combines cell culture and computer technology. The instrument can be used to screen new drugs, perform toxicity tests, or study disease processes.

close it is to the original. Scientists do not know everything about how body systems operate. Unknown factors cannot be programmed in.

Mathematical models are simplified versions of reality that are helpful in understanding complicated systems. They are especially helpful in cases in which several factors may affect the outcome. Once the model has been validated, or proven accurate, researchers can change one or more variables to see the response.

Charles DeLisi and coworkers at the National Cancer Institute used mathematical modeling to analyze the immune system's response to cancer. Their work showed that the immune system could stimulate cancer growth as well as fight it. "[I]f our model had been around ten years ago," says DeLisi, "it could have predicted what it's taken scientists countless man-hours and animals to figure out. This is the value of mathematical modeling—it comes up with things that you might otherwise miss."[4]

Computers can also help with "data mining," surveying existing data to look for patterns or connections. For example, Horst Spielmann of ZEBET, a center for alternatives to animal testing located in Germany, evaluated data on pesticides. He determined that if rats and mice are sensitive to a chemical, it is not necessary to test it on dogs. His findings mean that 70 percent of the dog tests can be eliminated.[5]

Instrumentation

In grandmother's time, she may have told her husband that they were expecting a child by saying, "the rabbit died." Before alternative pregnancy tests were developed, a female rabbit was injected with a sample of the woman's urine. After a period of time, the rabbit was killed, and its ovaries were checked for changes. In reality, the rabbit died whether the woman was pregnant or not. Now the urine sample can go to a laboratory where high-speed instrumentation is able to determine in minutes whether or not the couple should buy diapers.

Complex equipment can analyze the physical and chemical properties of drugs, toxins, body chemicals, and other substances. Instruments like high-performance liquid chromatographs and mass spectrophotometers can isolate, identify, and measure even the smallest amounts of chemicals in complex mixtures. Instruments have replaced animals in many vitamin assays and can help test drug potency.

Technologies that allow scientists to observe body processes without cutting the body open are another promising area of research. Some offer a way to measure chemical changes. Others provide a way to see inside the bodies of humans or animals without harming them. Magnetic resonance imaging (MRI), for example, uses magnetic fields and radio waves to create computer images of sections of the body. Using the fast MRI method, doctors can observe changes as they occur, allowing them to watch blood flow through the heart, evaluate liver function, even see the brain function. Using this form of imaging, doctors can visualize patients' thought patterns, which may lead to a better understanding of such complex problems as addiction, depression, and anxiety. As imaging becomes increasingly sophisticated, it is reducing the need to cut animals and humans open to see what is happening.

Developing New Alternatives

In 1981, Johns Hopkins University in Baltimore established the Center for Alternatives to Animal Testing (CAAT). Its vision is to "be a leading force in the development and use of reduction, refinement, and replacement alternatives in research, testing, and education to protect and enhance the health of the public."[6]

Working with and receiving funding from trade groups such as the Cosmetic, Toiletry, and Fragrance

Association, Inc., as well as individual corporations, CAAT has worked to help pharmaceutical and cosmetics companies find safe alternatives to animal testing. The center also disburses $1 million a year in grants toward developing alternatives to animal testing.

In 1998, CAAT started a program called *Vision 20/20*. It consists of representatives from industry, government, and animal welfare organizations who meet to discuss strategies for moving alternative methods into the marketplace more quickly.

Can Alternatives Completely Replace Animals?

Some animal activists believe that scientists are stalling. Neal Barnard says that the kinds of research that really need to be done do not involve animals. "So if the question is," says Barnard, " 'Can we get rid of animal experiments completely?,' my answer is 'yes.' "[7]

Most scientists disagree. "There's a public misconception," says Robert Phalen,

> that scientists are somehow real stupid compared to the lay people who attack science and that scientists are ignoring this wealth of study information that's right there that could answer all the questions. That is not true. The people I know that are scientists use absolutely every tool they can and they start with things like mathematical models, cell cultures, cadavers, human organs . . . but the animals are absolutely necessary. There are certain critical roles that they fulfill [for which] there are no other techniques.[8]

Steve Kaufman finds the scientists' criticisms unfair. "Many animal activists," says Kaufman, "recognize that the nonanimal methods often suffer from problems—as do the animal methods. But they are useful adjuncts. And there are many times that I wouldn't call them alternatives to animals. I would call them superior methods of research."[9]

Alan M. Goldberg, Ph.D., director of CAAT, says that proper science requires a combination of clinical, whole-animal, and in vitro studies. "You use one set of methodologies to raise you to a new level of understanding. And then you may have to go back and recycle through all of those methods again to raise you yet to other levels of understanding."[10]

Barnard does not even like to think in terms of alternatives.

> We don't want to imply that somehow animal experiments are the main line to progress and that everything else is an alternative, or second best. Rather, other research methods, I think, really have shown that they are far preferable to retreating from human health problems and looking into animals.[11]

Resistance to Alternative Technologies

Animal activists complain that the system is designed around animal models and is therefore actively resisting change. They say resistance comes from government regulatory agencies, research institutions, the scientists themselves, and a "we've always done it this way" mentality.

Kaufman says that many more alternatives could

be used if the regulatory agencies would approve them. But they are afraid to take the risk. Industry really does not have much incentive to change either, according to Kaufman. "They're afraid that the in vitro tests will just be added on to the animal tests and cost them money."[12]

Zawistowski agrees. "The difficulty with the testing question for consumer products," he says, "is as much a question of liability as it is of scientific validity." He recalls speaking with a company lawyer about using alternative tests. "Even if you could show me that animal data weren't needed," said the attorney, "I would still advise the president of the company to do animal testing—just in case something should happen, we could show we tried our best."[13]

Goldberg does not believe scientists are resisting alternatives. "Good science has a vested interest in trying to understand and contribute to society. And I know that my faculty and colleagues think of themselves as doing just that. So they're going to use the best methods that will advance our understandings of biology and society and help humans and nonhumans."[14]

Doing Without

One alternative to animal experimentation is simply to do without certain tests and eliminate some kinds of research. For instance, animal rights advocates question the need for military, psychological, addiction, and other studies done on animals.

The use of animals as organ donors could be eliminated if mechanical substitutes were developed or if human organs were in good supply. More human organs would be available if doctors were allowed to harvest human organs at death unless the person had previously registered an objection. Or cash incentives could be offered to individuals or their families to encourage donation.

A lot of animal testing and some animal research is conducted by companies hoping to come up with products to compete with other companies. It can be argued that such experimentation is unnecessary. Zawistowski asks, "At what level and when do you say we've got some pretty decent products for cleaning your sink out?"[15]

Barnard sees a similar pattern in the drug industry.

> The pharmaceutical houses are amongst the most profitable industries in America as well as in other countries, and most of the drugs that enter the market have nothing whatsoever to do with advancing human health. They have only to do with that company trying to get market share.[16]

Doing without another sink cleaner or a duplicated drug is one thing, but what about giving up a better treatment for a disease or a safer pesticide? Some sacrifices would not be easy. Would people accept a slightly higher risk of injury from a product if it saved animal lives? Should we stop animal research even if it means that there might be some diseases that could never be cured? More to the point, who decides?

Back to the Future

What do scientists and activists see in their crystal balls?

John Young says that he is seeing less "direct assault" from the animal activists, and more attempts to restrict animal research through legislative action. He points to an effort in New Zealand to grant human rights to great apes and says that American groups are attempting to attain legal standing so that they will be able to sue on behalf of individual animals. He believes that their real goal is simply to file so many lawsuits that animal research will grind to a halt.[17]

In 1999, two of America's top law schools, Harvard and Georgetown, announced that they would offer courses in animal law for the first time. While professor Richard A. Epstein of the University of Chicago Law School asked, "Would even bacteria have rights?" others said that the idea that animals are mere property developed centuries ago, when animals were not known to have perceptions or emotions. Steven M. Wise, who is scheduled to teach the animal law course at Harvard, said "It [legal work on behalf of animals] . . . is a long-term strategy to show that animals are not just things for our use."[18]

F. Barbara Orlans, of the Kennedy Institute of Ethics at Georgetown University, says that the battle between scientists and animal rights activists must end. Orlans says,

Animal liberators need to accept that animal research is beneficial to humans. And animal researchers need to admit that if animals are close enough to humans that their bodies, brains, and even psyches are good models for the human condition, then ethical dilemmas surely arise in using them.[19]

Michael Kirby does not see any alternatives to animals for his work. "Most of our techniques require the tissue from the baby," says Kirby,

so we'd actually have to go in and pull out part of its brain, and that simply can't be done on a human infant. . . . Down the road, it may be the case that we can actually do experiments in the infants without harming them—without having to take out that tissue—in which case then that would eliminate the use of animals and we could go more into a twenty-first, twenty-second century kind of medicine where we can actually visualize experiments within the infant without doing them any harm. But we're not there yet.[20]

Zawistowski says,

I think that what we'll see is testing that will go through a variety of first, chemical analyzes, then tissue culture analyzes, and then testing on humans, which occurs anyway. After they go through all of the animal tests, they still get a bunch of volunteers who come in and use the products. The question is to what extent animals are required in the interim—in that in-between spot.[21]

Interest in minimizing the numbers of animals used in research seems to be growing. When, in

October 1998, the Clinton Administration, the Environmental Defense Fund (EDF), and the Chemical Manufacturers Association launched a six-year program to test two thousand eight hundred major industrial chemicals to determine their health and environmental effects, it appeared that there would be an enormous increase in animals used for testing. By April 1999, CAAT, EDF, Carnegie-Mellon University, and the University of Pittsburgh had developed a collaborative effort called TestSmart, to work toward including in vitro and other alternatives, reducing the numbers of animals required for the project.

Young is concerned that animal activists are increasingly targeting young people with antiresearch propaganda. "Although I'm gratified to find out that most kids in grade school haven't been swayed one way or the other yet and are receptive to factual information, I see more and more high school kids that have preconceptions because of the literature they have in their libraries."[22]

Elizabeth Darrow feels that ending animal experimentation is possible only if animal activists and scientists work together. After PETA she worked for the Pure Food Campaign because, she says, they are trying to link animal activists with researchers and farmers to work toward a common solution. She advises students to

> try to look at the issues from every different perspective and gain as much information as you possibly can before you discover your own viewpoint or make up your own mind on the

subject. Really put yourself in everybody else's shoes and, in dealing with other people, listen respectfully to what they have to say and try to challenge your own assumptions and learn from what other people's views are.[23]

Decide for Yourself

The issue of using animals for medical research, education, and product testing is a complicated one. On one side are questions regarding the ethics of whether it is right to use nonhuman animals to serve humans, arguments as to whether animal experimentation has provided any benefits, and concerns as to the numbers of animals used for animal experimentation. On the other side are arguments that animal research has been and continues to be a vital part of our medical progress and that animal experimentation is needed to protect people from dangerous products and untried drugs, to educate students and train physicians, and to help scientists better understand disease and develop new medical treatments.

As proponents for each side continue to present arguments supporting their positions, it is important to take time to consider the validity of their claims. Read factual material (not just promotional literature), visit laboratories, hospitals, research institutions, and veterinary facilities; talk to experts on both sides of the issue. Then decide for yourself.

List of Abbreviations

AALAS—American Association for Laboratory Animal Science

AAVS—American Anti-Vivisection Society

ALF—Animal Liberation Front

AMA—American Medical Association

AMP—Americans for Medical Progress

ASPCA—American Society for the Prevention of Cruelty to Animals

CAAT—Center for Alternatives to Animal Testing

FDA—Food and Drug Administration

FTC—Federal Trade Commission

HSUS—The Humane Society of the United States

iiFAR—Incurably Ill for Animal Research

MRMC—Medical Research Modernization Committee

PCRM—Physicians Committee for Responsible Medicine

PETA—People for the Ethical Treatment of Animals

USDA—United States Department of Agriculture

Chapter Notes

Chapter 1. The Battleground

1. Ingrid Newkirk, *Free the Animals! The Untold Story of the U.S. Animal Liberation Front and Its Founder, "Valerie"* (Chicago: Noble Press, 1992), pp. 97–100.

2. Ken Ringle, "Cat Burglary: 'Animal Liberation Front' Says It Staged Raid on Howard U. Lab," *The Washington Post*, December 28, 1982, p. B1.

3. Phil McCombs, "Life and Death on the Cutting Edge: Researcher Steve Wilson and the Animal Rights Debate," *The Washington Post*, June 2, 1986, p. B1.

4. Office of Technology Assessment, "U.S. Congress. Alternatives to Animal Use in Research, Testing, and Education" (Washington, D.C.: U.S. Government Printing Office, 1986).

5. Erin Lindeman, "U. Pittsburgh Med School Dean Defends Medical Research," *The Pitt News*, via University Wire, January 26, 1999.

6. USDA, 1997 Animal Welfare Enforcement Report, 1998 USDA Animal Welfare Enforcement Report (preliminary figures), personal communication, April 13, 1999, Robert M. Gibbens, USDA Animal and Plant Health Inspection Service, Sacramento, California.

7. Chris DeRose, fax interview, August 23, 1999.

8. Valerie Richardson, "Animal Activists Add Bite to Effective Bark," *The Washington Times*, December 26, 1996, p. A1.

9. Colin Blakemore, "Sunday Comment: I Will Talk to Those Who Threaten to Murder Me. By Prof. Colin Blakemore, One of the Animal Rights Movement's Assassination Targets," *The Sunday Telegraph*, December 6, 1998, p. 37.

Chapter 2. Science and Experimentation

1. Rebecca Kolberg, "Animal Models Point the Way to Human Clinical Trials," *Science*, May 8, 1992, p. 772.

2. Richard McCourt, "Model Patients," *Discover*, August 1990, pp. 36–37.

3. Andrew N. Rowan, Franklin M. Loew, and Joan C. Weer, "The Animal Research Controversy: Protest, Process & Public Policy: An Analysis of Strategic Issues," Center for Animals & Public Policy, Tufts University School of Veterinary Medicine, 1995, p. 19.

4. Neal Barnard, telephone interview, May 3, 1993.

5. Barnard, telephone interview, April 14, 1999.

6. Elizabeth Darrow, telephone interview, May 3, 1993.

7. Ibid.

8. F. Barbara Orlans, *The Human Use of Animals: Case Studies in Ethical Choice* (New York: Oxford University Press, 1998), pp. 124, 126–127.

9. Stephen Kaufman, telephone interview, March 6, 1993.

10. Barbara Thomas, "Fashionable SoCal; Beauty; The Sign of Alternative Testing," *Los Angeles Times*, January 22, 1999, p. E3.

11. "Animal Testing," U.S. Food and Drug Administration, Center for Food Safety and Applied Nutrition, Office of Cosmetics Fact Sheet, February 3, 1995.

12. "Trials and Tribulations: More Effective Clinical Trials May Be Just Around the Corner," *The Economist*, vol. 346, February 21, 1998, p. S13.

13. Joseph C. Besharse, et al., "Redefining Rats, Mice, and Birds," *Science*, April 2, 1999, letter, p. 49.

14. Madhusree Mukerjee, "Trends in Animal Research," *Scientific American*, February 1997, p. 92.

15. Ibid.

16. Humane Society of the United States, "Population Facts at a Glance," Fact Sheet, 1999.

17. Robert Phalen, telephone interview, April 1, 1993.

Chapter 3. The History of Animal Experimentation

1. Jerod M. Loeb, William R. Hendee, Steven J. Smith, and M. Roy Schwarz, "Human vs. Animal Rights: In Defense of Animal Research," *JAMA*, November 17, 1989, p. 2717.

2. Kenneth L. Feder and Michael Alan Park, "Animal Rights: An Evolutionary Perspective," *The Humanist*, July/August 1990, p. 7.

3. Andrew N. Rowan, *Of Mice, Models, and Men: A Critical Evaluation of Animal Research* (Albany: State University of New York Press, 1984), p. 51.

4. Susan Sperling, *Animal Liberators: Research & Morality* (Berkeley: University of California Press, 1988), p. 81.

5. F. Barbara Orlans, *The Human Use of Animals: Case Studies in Ethical Choice* (New York: Oxford University Press, 1998), pp. 55–64.

6. John Young, telephone interview, April 14, 1999.

7. "Of Pigs, Primates, and Plagues: A Layperson's Guide to the Problems With Animal-to-Human Organ Transplants," *Medical Research Modernization Committee*, DATE.

8. Young, April 14, 1999.

9. Kathleen Kerr, "Fit for Humans? Genetically Altered Pigs Show Promise for Organ Transplants," *Newsday*, April 27, 1999, p. C3.

10. Bruce Wallace, "Special Report: The Dolly Debate: A Sheep Cloned in Scotland Raises Hopes and Fears About a Fantastic Technology," *Macleans*, March 10, 1997, p. 54.

11. Valerie Richardson, "Animal Activists Add Bite to Effective Bark," *The Washington Times*, December 26, 1996, p. A1.

12. Brad Knickerbocker, "Activists Step Up War to 'Liberate' Nature," *The Christian Science Monitor*, January 20, 1999, p. 4.

13. Tim Reid, "Why I Quit the Evil Animal Fanatics: 'They Don't Really Care About Wildlife and They Hate Humans,'" *The Sunday Telegraph*, August 16, 1998, p. 12.

Chapter 4. The Ethical Issues

1. Ann Gibbons, "Comparative Genetics: Which of Our Genes Make Us Human?" *Science*, September 4, 1998, p. 1432.

2. Steven Zak, "Ethics and Animals," *The Atlantic Monthly*, March 1989, p. 71.

3. Heather Jensen, "Speaking Up for Creepy-Crawlies: The Speciesism Debate," *Daily Utah Chronicle*, via University Wire, October 20, 1998.

4. "Conference Explores Ethics of Animal Research With Critical Thinking and Balanced Argument," *JAMA*, July 10, 1996, pp. 87–88.

5. Peter Singer, *Animal Liberation*, 2nd ed. (New York: Random House, 1990), pp. 8–9.

6. Tom Regan (letter), "Is Justification of Animal Research Necessary?" *JAMA*, March 3, 1993, p. 1113.

7. Margaret L. Knox, "The Rights Stuff," Buzzworm, May/June 1991, p. 36.

Chapter 5. The Case Against Animal Experimentation

1. Hugh LaFollette and Niall Shanks, *Brute Science: Dilemmas of Animal Experimentation* (London: Routledge, 1996), pp. 236–237.

2. Stephen Zawistowski, telephone interview, May 14, 1993.

3. Neal Barnard, telephone interview, May 3, 1993.

4. Stephen Kaufman, telephone interview, March 6, 1993.

5. Neal Barnard and Stephen Kaufman, "Animal Research Is Wasteful and Misleading," *Scientific American*, February, 1997, p. 80.

6. Ibid., p. 82.

7. Barnard, May 3, 1993.

8. Ibid.

9. Kaufman, March 6, 1993.

10. Katie McCabe, "Who Will Live, Who Will Die?" *The Washingtonian*, August 1986, p. 118.

11. Zawistowski, May 14, 1993.

12. Kaufman, telephone interviews, March 6, 1993, April 14, 1999.

13. Zawistowski, May 14, 1993.

14. Elizabeth Darrow, telephone interview, May 3, 1993.

15. Barnard, May 3, 1993.

Chapter 6. The Case for Animal Experimentation

1. Erin Lindeman, "U. Pittsburgh Med School Dean Defends Medical Research," *The Pitt News*, via University Wire, January 26, 1999.

2. American Medical Association, "Use of Animals in Biomedical Research: The Challenge and Response," *AMA* white paper, 1992, p. 11.

3. Polly Toynbee, "The Relative Value of Mice and Men," *Independent*, December 10, 1996, p. 15.

4. Jack H. Botting and Adrian R. Morrison, "Animal Research is Vital to Medicine," *Scientific American*, February 1997, p. 83.

5. Robert Phalen, telephone interview, April 1, 1993.

6. Murray Gardner, telephone interview, April 19, 1999.

7. Michael Kirby, telephone interview, April 12, 1999.

8. Ibid.

9. National Agricultural Statistics Service: Livestock Slaughter, Poultry Slaughter, M2 PressWIRE, February 22, 1999.

10. Phalen, April 1, 1993, p.72.

11. John G. Hubbell, "The 'Animal Rights' War on Medicine," *Reader's Digest*, June 1990, p. 72.

12. John Young, telephone interview, April 13, 1993.

13. American Medical Association, "Use of Animals in Biomedical Research," p. 23.

14. Gardner, April 19, 1999.

15. Charles M. Balch, W. Archie Bleyer, Irwin H. Krakoff, and Lester J. Peters, "The Vital Role of Animal Research in Advancing Cancer Diagnosis and Treatment," *The Cancer Bulletin*, vol. 42, no. 4 (1990), p. 268.

16. Hubbell, p. 73.

17. Ankur Desai, "Animal Rights Debate Rages on Berkeley Campus," *The Daily Californian*, via University Wire, March 16, 1998.

18. Michael Kirby, telephone interview, April 16, 1993.

19. Frankie L. Trull, *USA Today*, March 1988, p. 52 ff. as reprinted in *Animal Rights & Welfare*, ed. Jeanne Williams (New York: Wilson, 1991), p. 64.

20. Philip Johnston, "A Long and Bitter Battle Over Beauty and the Beasts. Of 22.6 Million Experiments Last Year, Only 1,300 Were by Companies Making Cosmetics," *The Daily Telegraph*, November 17, 1998, p. 4.

Chapter 7. Experimentation on Humans

1. National Public Radio, "Acres of Skin," *NPR*, July 28, 1998.

2. M. H. Pappworth, *Human Guinea Pigs: Experimentation on Man* (Boston: Beacon Press, 1968), pp. 68–70.

3. Katie McCabe, "Who Will Live, Who Will Die?" *The Washingtonian*, August 1986, p. 116.

4. Pappworth, pp. 34–35.

5. Gerald L. Posner and John Ware, *Mengele: The Complete Story* (New York: McGraw-Hill, 1986), pp. 29–44.

6. James H. Jones, *Bad Blood: The Tuskegee Syphilis Experiment* (New York: Free Press, 1993), p. 10.

7. Tom Regan, "The Case for Animal Rights," *Animal Experimentation: The Moral Issues*, Robert M. Baird and Stuart E. Rosenbaum, eds. (Buffalo, New York: Prometheus Books, 1991), pp. 83–84.

8. Sheryl Gay Stolberg, "Decisive Moment on Parkinson's Fetal-Cell Transplants," *The New York Times*, April 20, 1999, p. F2.

9. Nicholas Wade, "Government Says Ban on Human Embryo Research Does Not Apply to Cells," *The New York Times*, January 20, 1999, p. A29.

10. U.S. Department of Health and Human Services. "Fact Sheet on Stem Cell Research," *M2 PressWIRE*, February 1, 1999.

11. Eliot Marshall, "Clinical Research: Shutdown of Research at Duke Sends a Message," *Science*, May 21, 1999, p. 1246.

12. Robert Pear. "Study Finds Risks to Patients in Drug Trials," *The New York Times*, May 30, 1998, p. A9.

13. Stolberg, p. F2.

14. "Trials and Tribulations: More Effective Clinical Trials May Be Just Around the Corner," *The Economist*, vol. 346, February 21, 1998, p. S13.

15. John H. Cushman Jr., "Group Wants Pesticide Companies to End Testing on Humans," *The New York Times*, July 28, 1998, p. A9.

16. Robert Phalen, telephone interview, April 1, 1993.

17. Tom Regan, *The Case for Animal Rights* (Berkeley: University of California Press, 1983), p. .

Chapter 8. The Alternatives

1. Michael Kirby, telephone interview, April 12, 1999.

2. Andrew Pollack, "Drug Testers Turn to 'Virtual Patients' as Guinea Pigs," *The New York Times*, November 10, 1998, p. F1.

3. Ibid., p. F10.

4. Natalie Angier, "The Electronic Guinea Pig," *Discover*, September 1983, p. 80.

5. Madhusree Mukerjee, "Trends in Animal Research," *Scientific American*, February 1997, p. 90.

6. Vision Statement, Johns Hopkins University Center for Alternatives to Animal Testing, March 3, 1998 <http://www.jhsph.edu/~caat/caat.html> (April 20, 1999).

7. Neal Barnard, telephone interview, April 14, 1999.

8. Robert Phalen, telephone interview, April 1, 1993.

9. Stephen Kaufman, telephone interview, March 6, 1993.

10. Alan Goldberg, telephone interview, May 14, 1993.

11. Barnard, April 14, 1999.

12. Kaufman, March 6, 1993.

13. Stephen Zawistowski, telephone interview, May 14, 1993.

14. Goldberg, May 14, 1993.

15. Zawistowski, May 14, 1993.

16. Barnard, telephone interview, May 3, 1993.

17. John Young, telephone interview, April 14, 1999.

18. William Glaberson, "Legal Pioneers Seek to Raise Lowly Status of Animals," *The New York Times*, August 18, 1999, pp. A1, A18.

19. Mukerjee, p. 93.

20. Kirby, April 16, 1993.

21. Zawistowski, May 14, 1993.

22. Young, April 14, 1999.

23. Elizabeth Darrow, telephone interview, April 6, 1999.

Glossary

animal rights advocates—People who believe that animals have rights, including the right not to be experimented on or to be used by humans for their own purposes.

animal welfare advocates—People who believe that animals should receive humane care and treatment.

antivivisection—Opposition to the use of live animals for experimentation, specifically, for experimentation that involves any cutting operation.

cell culture—Living cells from humans or animals, maintained in a nutrient fluid, used for study and experimentation.

clinical trials—Tests on human volunteers. New drugs or treatments are tried on a limited group of human subjects after animal testing and before release to the public.

cloning—Producing an individual from a single cell of one parent and thereby creating a genetically identical twin of the parent.

Draize—A scale used to measure the degree of skin or eye irritation caused by test substances. Tests are usually conducted using rabbits.

epidemiological studies—Analyzing information obtained by studying disease as it affects groups of people, as opposed to individuals.

euthanized—Killed painlessly.

in vitro—"In glass," or processes occurring in the laboratory rather than in the body.

in vivo—"In the living being," or processes occurring in the body.

induced models—Models that have been created by modifying animals in some way so they provide a way to study a disease or condition.

informed consent—Before a medical procedure or test, the human subject is given a full explanation. Then the subject is asked whether he or she understands the procedure and the risks involved and is asked to indicate his or her willing consent to it by signing a consent form.

model—A representation of something; in this book, an animal or other substitute that represents the human body for the purposes of research or testing.

pounds—Public facilities for stray or unwanted animals.

reproducible—Something that can be repeated; in this book, experiments that, when copied by other scientists, using the same materials and methods, yield the same results.

scientific method—Principles and procedures for pursuing scientific knowledge, which include formulating a problem, gathering information through observation and experimentation, and creating and testing theories.

sentient—Conscious of sense impressions such as pain.

shelters—Facilities run by organizations such as the ASPCA to house stray and unwanted animals.

species—A biological classification of related organisms that can breed with one another.

speciesism—Prejudice or discrimination based on species, specifically, discrimination against animals.

spontaneous models—Animals that naturally develop diseases or conditions that scientists wish to study.

Three Rs—Russell's and Burch's goals of humane experimentation: reduction, refinement, and replacement. These goals were to reduce the numbers of animals used in experiments, refine the methods of animal experimentation so that suffering is minimized and the knowledge gained is maximized, and find other methods to replace the use of animals.

toxicity—The property of being poisonous. Toxicity testing is conducted to determine whether and to what degree chemicals are hazardous.

utilitarian argument—The ethical position that decisions should be made based on the best balance of good and bad results for everyone involved.

variable—That which changes. In an experiment, the uncontrolled variable is the one factor that varies.

vivisection—Experimentation on living animals, usually experimentation that involves cutting.

xenotransplantation—The use of live animal cells, tissues, or organs in human bodies. Often used to refer to the transplantation of an animal organ into a human patient.

Further Reading

Harnack, Andrew, ed. *Animal Rights: Opposing Viewpoints*. San Diego, Calif.: Greenhaven Press, 1996.

Haugen, David M. *Animal Experimentation*. San Diego, Calif.: Greenhaven Press, 1999.

Hurley, Jennifer A. *Animal Rights*. San Diego, Calif.: Greenhaven Press, 1998.

James, Barbara. *Animal Rights*. Orlando, Fla.: Raintree Steck-Vaughn, 1999.

Levine, Herbert M. *Animal Rights*. Orlando, Fla.: Raintree Steck-Vaughn, 1997.

Owen, Marna A. *Animal Rights—Yes or No*. Minneapolis: Lerner Publications, 1993.

Roleff, Tamara L. and Jennifer A. Hurley. *The Rights of Animals*. San Diego, Calif.: Greenhaven Press, 1999.

Woods, Geraldine. *Animal Experimentation and Testing: A Pro/Con Issue*. Springfield, N.J.: Enslow Publishers, 1999.

Internet Addresses

American Anti-Vivisection Society (AAVS)

<http://www.aavs.org>

An international organization that works to end the use of animals in biomedical research, dissection, testing, and education.

American Association for Laboratory Animal Science (AALAS)

<http://www.aalas.org>

An organization that promotes the advancement of responsible laboratory animal care and use.

The Humane Society of the United States (HSUS)

<http://www.hsus.org/programs/research/index.html>

The mission of their Animal Research Issues section is to reduce and eventually eliminate harm to animals used in research, testing, and education through the promotion of alternate testing methods.

Incurably Ill for Animal Research

<http://www.iifar.org>

This organization supports animal experimentation. It consists of people who have health problems and are concerned that animal research will be stopped or limited due to the efforts of animal rights activists.

People for the Ethical Treatment of Animals (PETA)

<http://www.peta-online.org>

PETA opposes all forms of animal exploitation, including using animals for food, clothing, entertainment, and experimentation.

Physicians Committee for Responsible Medicine (PCRM)

<http://www.pcrm.org>

This organization is against animal experimentation for research purposes.

Index